cyber writing

cyber writing

How to Promote Your Product or
Service Online (without being flamed)

Joe Vitale

amacom
American Management Association
New York · Atlanta · Boston · Chicago · Kansas City · San Francisco · Washington, D.C.
Brussels · Mexico City · Tokyo · Toronto

Library of Congress Cataloging-in-Publication Data

Vitale, Joseph G.
    Cyber writing : how to promote your product or service online
    (without being flamed) / Joe Vitale.
        p.   cm.
    Includes index.
    ISBN 0-8144-7918-9
    1. Internet marketing.   2. Internet advertising.   I. Title.
HF4515.1265.V58   1996
659.1'0285'467—dc20   96-8276
                                                                    CIP

Printing number

10   9   8   7   6   5   4   3   2   1

For
Syndi

"Once sent out a word takes wing irrevocably."
—Horace

Contents

Foreword: You Are What You Write

by Charles Rubin

Writing ability is the single most important weapon you can wield in cyberspace. The words you write are your best and often only chance to create an impression on customers. Just as your confidence in an offline vendor is affected by that person's command of the language, your prospects' opinion of you in cyberspace is affected by your command of the written word. Before you will ever have the chance to impress customers with your superior service, expertise, or follow-up, many of your prospects will decide whether or not to do business with you by the quality of your written communications.

None of us like to think our writing skills need improving, and even fewer of us are willing to spend the time and energy to improve them. But consider this: Your larger and better-financed competitors pay professional writers to create their storefront copy, produce electronic publications and brochures, and perhaps even compose their e-mail for them. In order to compete, you must develop the same professionalism in your writing. Professionalism in writing means:

Correctness. Messages filled with errors tell everyone that you don't care enough about your online presence to get it right. Strive to eliminate spelling, grammatical, and formatting errors from all your online messages. If you can't spot the errors, have someone else proofread your text.

Clarity. Use words that say exactly what you mean to say. Vague or ambiguous messages cause confusion that will either abort a budding business relationship entirely or force you to waste time sending further messages before making your point.

Economy. Say what you have to say in as little space as possible. Nobody in cyberspace has enough time, so any message that wastes time automatically gets a negative reception. Respect your prospects' and customers' time by keeping messages brief and to the point.

Personality. Infuse as much of your business identity into a message as possible, and speak directly to the individual reader. Use the same words and figures of speech you use in day-to-day conversation, and envision a specific person as your correspondent whenever you write something. The pros also know that using words like "you," "we," "us," and "our" makes a message much more personal. Everyone who reads your message should feel as if the message is directed specifically at him or her.

So rather than dashing off messages without a second thought, give your writing the same care and consideration you would use in designing a print ad or reviewing the copy for a printed brochure. It means an extra investment of time, but the payoff will be a better online presence, higher customer confidence, and a fatter bottom line.

If you want to write to sell online, and reap all the financial rewards of doing it right, then this is the book you want in your guerrilla arsenal. Read it and reread it. I did.

Charles Rubin
Coauthor, *Guerrilla Marketing Online*
and *Guerrilla Marketing Online Weapons*

crubin@sedona.net
http://www.sedona.net/crubin

Acknowledgments

This book was the idea of my agent, Nicholas Smith. I thank him for his encouragement and support throughout the process of developing this book. I also want to thank my friends who took the time to review the manuscript and help me shape it into the form you now hold: Penny Perez, Jim King, Scott Hammaker, Connie Schmidt, Ron Kaye, Mark Weisser, Cliff Kurtzman, Larry Weinstein, Blair Warren, Tom Mulkern, Greg Manning, and John Martin.

I want to thank Cliff Kurtzman of the Tenagra Corporation for giving me my introduction to the Internet, Marc Newman of the Black Box for putting me online, Daniel Kehoe of Fortuity Consulting for sponsoring my first web pages, Larry Weinstein for his always enthusiastic support, David Deutsch for his sharing of information, Claudia Robinson for her online research, and Marian, my wife, for watching me spend night and day online without a moment's complaint.

cyber writing

Introduction: Three Reasons You Need This Book Today

Like it or not, cyberspace is going to change the way you do business. Whether you make extensive use of this new opportunity or not, you will be affected by your more cyber-savvy competitors. Just look at your local newspaper. The analysts agree: The companies that will be successful in the future will be the companies that learn, use, and exploit the power of the online world.

Many people view cyberspace as little more than the electronic equivalent of a giant newspaper or clubhouse. Yet nothing could be further from the truth. Cyberspace is an entirely new, extremely powerful medium, where the old rules of writing, marketing, and social etiquette no longer apply. To make it online, you must learn what is and what is not understandable; what does and does not sell; and what is and is not acceptable. If you don't, you and your message are doomed.

Are you already online? Good. Because this book isn't a travel guide or a technical manual. Rather, it is for those of us who have already logged on to cyberspace and now want to know how to best communicate there. As you may have already discovered, writing online is different from writing on paper. How? In at least three ways—and those three ways also happen to be exactly why you need this book.

What Looks Good on Paper Rarely Looks Good Onlin and Vice Versa

This paragraph looks fine on this paper and in this bool upload and e-mail this very same paragraph to a friend may end up looking something like the one on the next

```
This paragraph looks fine on this paper
and in
this book. But up
load
and e-mail this very same paragraph to a friend and
it may end
up
looking
something
like this:
```

What happened?

Since ASCII text is the universal language of cyberspace, everything you send gets reduced to an ASCII format. ASCII is a bare-bones font with virtually no frills. That means that nearly all embellishments, fonts, font sizes, graphics, underlining—even your margins—get wiped out, and what's left often gets rearranged to fit the receiver's screen.

And that's not all. Everyone online uses different computers. Some have Macs; others have PCs. Still others may use a laptop, or even a small palmtop computer or information manager. Also, many of these users may select different fonts and font sizes for their incoming electronic messages. This all means that what looks great on your screen is likely to get chopped up to fit someone else's smaller or different screen.

So what? What does it matter if your words get rearranged? Well, imagine that your secretary types up one of your letters in the form of an e. e. cummings poem: no capital letters, irregular lines, and no logic to its structure. Not only would you look foolish and very unprofessional, you would probably lose sales—even customers! If your business letters are hard to look at and hard to read while your competition's are flawless, who do you think will get the business?

There's more. Some people have **shell accounts,** which means that all they can see on screen is text, so none of your graphics will show up on a shell access user's screen. In place of r graphics all the user will see is the word "image." And e there are many popular **web browsers,** or online graphics ms, in use, they aren't alike. So what looks visually appealing on one screen using one web browser may look terrible on another.

Add to all of this the sad truth that most people don't know how to write to effectively communicate *anywhere* and you get a sense of the problem in cyberspace. At least in the real world businesspeople usually have an associate or secretary review and correct their words before they release them to the public. Online people tend to zip off e-messages without even stopping to double-check their spelling, let alone to check their content or message.

I heard of one executive who got angry because someone e-mailed him a note saying "I resent the last message." Why, the executive wondered, did he resent it? He felt confused and even insulted. It wasn't until several messages later that he discovered the word should have been "re-sent," as in "I re-*sent* the last message."

How do you compensate for all of these variables when writing online?

This book will tell you.

The "Ambiguity of Intention" Makes Accurate Communication Nearly Impossible

Face-to-face communication has the benefit of visual cues to help us understand our intended messages. If I say to you, "Your shirt had a stain on it this morning," and I smile and put my hand gently on your shoulder as I say it, you'll feel that I'm a trusted friend looking out for your well-being. If I send you a letter saying, "Your shirt had a stain on it in the meeting this morning," you'll probably assume the best: that I am trying to help you look good on the job.

But online, something happens when I e-mail you the identical message: Somehow, the cold letters on the emotionless screen seem to communicate the worst. Unfortunately, people reading online text often assume that your words are meant in a sarcastic, negative, or even abusive way. What the screen doesn't communicate is your true intention, and as you can imagine, this can be very bad for you. If you send an e-message saying "You need my product," people are likely to read that they are somehow lacking and you are gleefully pointing out that they need help.

I once sent an e-message to an associate saying "Thanks a lot for your help." But he somehow picked up a sarcastic and ironic tone, as in "Thanks a *lot* for your help!" Without my facial cues, he didn't realize I was sincerely thanking him for his contribution, so instead of feeling acknowledged, he felt offended. In fact, he was angry for several days until the matter was cleared up.

How would you like it if the electronic messages you send out, and the e-ads you post, insulted your prospects? Do you think it would help or hurt your business?

How do you get around this?

This book will tell you.

Online, Text Rules

If you can't write to communicate, you're dead.

Vince Gelormine, in *The Internet Marketing BlackBook*, reveals that fewer than 15 percent of the estimated 50 million people online have web browsers, meaning that the majority of people can only see *text* online. While this is changing by the nanosecond, the reality is that very few users can see graphics online. Even those with web browsers are quickly learning that graphics online are not all they are cracked up to be.

When I first went online in 1987 I used a 300 BPS modem. I thought I broke the sound barrier when I upgraded to a 1200 BPS. Today you'd better have a 28,800 BPS modem, or else have plenty to do while the graphics download to your computer. Some graphics take seven minutes to download at 28.8 BPS! That's a long wait in cyberspace—particularly when most of the pictures aren't worth waiting to see anyway. (Very often they are just company logos that no one but the company executives care about.)

When all is said and done, it's the words on screen that make you buy, reply, or move on. Not knowing how to write online is like trying to sell cars in Germany without knowing how to speak German. Since you can't touch or feel whatever is being described, your words alone have to work to make your product, service, or message come to life in your readers' minds. Online, text rules.

But the problem doesn't stop there. Generally speaking, users do not like to see advertisements online. There exists an old school mentality that says the Internet is for information exchange only. While this old guard is crumbling and changing, the fact remains that the vast majority of people online not only despise blatant and inappropriate advertising but will also let you know just how *much* they hate it. Since they are online, they can easily fire off to you, your competitors, your customers, your prospects—and even the press—e-mail messages that could give you nightmares for the rest of your life.

How do you write to sell online and not get flamed?

This book will tell you.

The Prime Directive of CyberSpace

Before we begin, I want to introduce a "prime directive" for your journey through this relatively new frontier.

The nature of the online world is such that people are often ruder, more obnoxious, less understanding, and less tolerant than in real life. Imagine Dennis the Menace or Bart Simpson at the keyboard, and you get the idea. There seems to be heightened miscommunication as well.

For example, I was a member of a marketing e-mailing list. The discussion was multi-level marketing, or MLM, a very volatile subject. One day I posted a message suggesting that people read a certain book on MLM by Richard Poe, a journalist. The next day someone posted a message saying Poe wasn't an objective journalist because he was a member of an MLM. I corrected that post with one of my own saying Poe was not in any MLM. The very next day someone else shot back, "If Poe isn't in an MLM, how can he write a book on it?" I could see this was a losing battle, so I quit contributing my comments.

I often feel that many people online post messages purposely to cause friction. One day someone accused me of posting messages just to get clients. No matter what I said, this perso was convinced I was a cyberspace criminal. Another time I s gested people read an article I had seen. Three people replied that I was blatantly advertising the article.

People who would never think of arguing with you face-to-face or interrupting you at a dinner party will write posts with a keyboard warmed up in hell. Personal attacks are common. One man suggested the group read a book by John Naisbitt. Someone else posted a message saying, "You obviously never read the book!" And someone else said, "Why should we? Just because he's an author doesn't make him smart!"

The computer hides the criminal but not the crime. Virginia Shea, in her book, *Netiquette*, suggests that the number one rule online should be "Remember the human."

It's too easy to fire off messages without stopping to consider that a real person with real feelings will read them. I've dropped out of discussion groups because of this coldness. I, too, have posted messages that were pretty harsh, which I later regretted writing.

I suggest that you and I carry a new prime directive with us as we traverse cyberspace. While I could say, "Remember the human," you might choose to remember how vicious that human was and still write something you'll regret. While I could say, "Do no harm," it might still be easy for you to write something that you think is harmless, yet brings the recipient to tears. Instead, I vote that we have a new prime directive. *Star Trek's* Captain James T. Kirk had his, I have mine:

"Write in kindness."

Before you start typing, consider: Are you writing out of kindness or from some other feeling? One day I was about to load and fire a message to a fellow who had been abusive to several people online. Before I began writing I stopped, took a deep breath, and asked myself, "Am I writing out of kindness?" No, I decided. Okay. How would I write—or would I even write—if I were responding out of kindness? I decided it was pointless to try to talk to this person, and I let it go. In this case, writing in kindness meant not writing at all.

As you journey through cyberspace, keep our new prime

directive in mind. If you encounter Romulans or other harsh life forms, do not despair. There are good souls out there who simply want to learn, experience, discover, and do business. Follow the prime directive and you will do well.

1

Five Basic Ways to Grab Attention in CyberSpace

In 1995, New York author Michael Wolff posted well over 100 messages about his new book online. Every one of them was deleted by someone calling himself "Cancelmoose." This unknown editor used a software program called "Cancelbot" to remove the posts. This is not uncommon. Online readers are not only remarkably sensitive to advertisements (and just as insensitive to the feelings of those who write them), they often react to them violently. Usually you "only" receive a **flame,** or hate e-mail. Sometimes you receive death threats. Or, in the case of Wolff, you may actually get flamed, receive death threats, *and* see your posts erased.

Imagine turning on your computer, logging online, and checking your e-mail. You are shocked to see a message that says:

> You *!*#xx!! Don't advertise your company business online!

That's a flame. Or imagine reading a message that says:

> You obviously don't know anything about your business. Where did you go to school? Or did you?

That's a flame as well. And as you can imagine, these flames can get hotter than what I can print here.

What can you do about this? How can you be sure you or your e-posts won't be destroyed by some anonymous online guard?

Here are five basic places for writing about your product or service online. Since these seem to be the fundamental means of communication online, let's discuss them first, before actually discovering how to write to sell. Knowing these basics will be the foundation for your learning how to create cyberwriting that keeps away the flames.

First Way: Usenet, Bulletin Boards to the World

Usenet groups are forums, news groups, special interest groups, or discussion areas centering around a common topic. There are over 10,000 Usenet groups online, most of which can be read by any online user, no matter what commercial online service he or she may be accessing. America Online, CompuServe, and many other large commercial online services have their own forums that you can only access if you are a member of their services. To make this book most useful to the most people, I'll focus on the Usenet groups that anyone online can access.

How to Find Usenet Groups

If for some reason your access to Usenet is limited, simply **telnet,** or telephone connect through your online service to a remote computer, to a site called:

```
launchpad.unc.ed
```

At your online prompt, type:

```
telnet launchpad.unc.edu
```

Once there, you'll be assigned an e-mail address and a password and given full access to more Usenet groups than you'll ever have time to read.

One way to learn more about Usenet is by sending e-mail to *mail-server@rtfm.mit.edu* and in the body of your message write:

```
send Usenet/news.answers/news-newusers-intro
```

If you want to actually receive the lists of Usenet groups available, send e-mail to the same address but this time write in the body of the message,

```
send Usenet/news.answers/active-newsgroups/part1
```

or visit the search engine Deja News at:

/http://www.dejanews.com

You'll find Usenet groups titled everything from *alt.sex* and *alt.make.money.now* to *sci.cryonics* and *soc.couples.* You'll quickly learn that many of these groups are a waste of time, filled with nothing but bickering and complaining posts. A little exploring will turn up the right groups for your messages. Unless your product or service has something to do with oversized purple extinct animals, don't post anything in *alt.barney.dinosaur,* or its evil sister group, *alt.barney.dinosaur.die.* Find the appropriate group for you. Here are several ways to target the best groups for your business:

1. Read *The Internet Resource Quick Reference* (Que Publications, 1994). This handy guide lists hundreds of resources, including Usenet groups, on the Internet.

2. Send an e-mail request to your **sysop** (system operator) and ask how you can access the Usenet groups on your online service.

3. When you are online and in the section for Usenet groups, try typing in what you think the Usenet group you want would be titled. For example, when I was worried about a health problem and wanted medical information, I searched for a Usenet group that could help me by typing in *sci.med.,* short for science-medicine. When I was hunting for an out-of-print book on marketing, I typed in *rec.books,* which led me to *rec.arts. books.marketplace,* a forum for sellers of out-of-print books.

4. Read the group *news.newusers.questions* to ask questions and learn more about Usenet groups.

Decoding Usenet

Usenet groups begin with different lowercase initials, and each abbreviation stands for something you should be aware of to help you locate the groups for you.

alt.   Any group beginning with *alt.* is an alternative discussion group. You'll find everything under the sun listed here, many of which will be controversial and/or ridiculous. Examples include *alt.sex.bondage* or *alt.fan.oj-simpson.*

biz.   These are business groups and probably where you'll find your home. If you're seeking a job, look in *biz.jobs.offered.*

comp.   Anything dealing with computers will fall into this category. For example, *comp.unix.questions* is an area for getting answers to the complex UNIX operating system.

misc.   Anything goes because this is for miscellaneous discussions.

news.   Here you'll find groups offering news, answers to new users questions, and other online news-oriented posts. To find a list of new Usenet groups, look in *news.lists.*

rec.   These are areas for exchanges on recreational topics, such as *rec.sport.boxing* or *rec.sport.rowing.*

sci.   Science groups begin with this prefix. They include *sci.space* and *sci.med.dentistry.*

soc.   These groups focus on social issues, such as *soc.feminisim,* and cultural discussions, such as *soc.culture.italian.*

talk.   You can debate anything you want in these long-winded Usenet groups, such as *talk.politics.guns.*

Finally, you may also find Usenet groups for your state or city. A group beginning with *tx* (without the capital letters) is for Texas. Something titled *houston* may be of interest to readers who, like me, live in Houston.

Sample Page of Usenet Groups

You won't want to subscribe to every newsgroup. There are too many of them. First, scan all the available groups by using your online service provider's command. (Ask your sysop how to do this.) Then browse all the group titles and subscribe to the ones you are interested in. Figure 1–1 is an example of a page of Usenet groups to which I currently subscribe.

How to Post on Usenet

Next, spend some time reading the posts in the Usenet group (or groups) you're interested in. Do not jump right in and post anything without becoming familiar with the style and personality of the group. As advertising legend Leo Burnett once said, "It seems axiomatic that you have to make a friend before you can effectively make him a proposition."

Don't crash any online parties. Become a friend to the groups. One of the first things you should do is find the FAQ file for the group you're interested in. A **FAQ** is a post of "frequently asked questions." It irritates netties to see you ask a question that has been posted a hundred times before. It also makes you look foolish. Browse the groups' posts, read the messages, and look for the FAQ. If you can't find it, post a message asking for it. If one exists, you'll be told privately (by e-mail) or publicly (by a post to the newsgroup) how to locate it.

Figure 1-1

```
 Group Selection (news.blkbox.com  10 R)        h=help

   1   1008   alt.business.misc
   2    813   misc.entrepreneurs
   3     30   alt.hypnosis
   4    348   rec.arts.books.marketplace
   5    356   rec.music.makers.guitar.acoustic
   6    238   rec.music.makers.songwriting
   7     18   misc.entrepreneurs.moderated
   8    156   alt.business.multilevel
   9   1066   alt.guitar.tab
  10      8   alt.psychology.nlp

              *** End of Groups ***
```

By reading the FAQ and following the thread of messages, you'll grasp what is important to the group. You can then compose a post that will be of interest to them and grab their attention. Here are four ways to do just that:

1. *Offer something of relevance free.* When I wanted to get the attention of online entrepreneurs, I found the Usenet group called *alt.entrepreneurs,* and another one called *alt.entrepreneurs. moderated* (Most Usenet groups do not have moderators; the ones that do have an individual who reads every message before it is posted and can decide to delete it if he or she feels the post is inappropriate for that group.) I posted a simple message that had the headline "FREE Marketing Articles!" The post itself said I was new to the group and was offering several of my marketing columns to anyone who sent me e-mail and asked for them. This was a powerful way to get attention for my work. Now that I've been online for years, I would not post a message with such a hyped-up headline. Instead, I would use the title from one of my marketing articles as the headline, such as "How to Write a Million-Dollar Letter." And if that still seemed too much like hype for whatever group I was about to post it to, I might change the headline to "How to Write a More Effective Marketing Letter." As you'll soon note, people online want solid information, not hype.

2. *Offer advice or opinions.* Don't be afraid to speak out. If you want to give your two cents regarding an issue of discussion on the group, do so. Posting messages online usually makes people more aggressive and vocal, mainly because of the safe anonymity of being unseen as you type. Carefully consider what you want to say, then write your message, and check it twice before posting it. Don't ever post a message you may regret later. Remember, what you write may be read by hundreds, even thousands, of people. They will judge you and your expertise on your post. Offer your thoughts, but offer them thoughtfully.

3. *Post a questionnaire.* Surveys and questionnaires are a proven way to gain attention for you and your business while gathering information about the people in the group. Be sure your questions are well thought out, stimulating, and even fun.

Anything that looks like a blatant attempt to make a sale will get you flamed. Sometimes a simple question may be the most effective way to go. If you're a consultant who writes marketing plans, asking, "How many here know how to write a marketing plan?" may unearth all kinds of people who desperately need your help.

4. *Post news.* The Usenet groups want news. That's why people read them. If you have news that pertains to the interests of the people reading the messages, post it. I know of one fellow who posts a press release every week concerning all the news he discovered that week that would be of interest to the group. His posts are a regular thing and have established him as an expert in his field. This authority status brings him a lot of new business from netties.

Sample Usenet Page

Figure 1–2 shows a sample directory page from the Usenet group *alt.business.misc.* As you can see, posts are first seen by headline and author. If readers aren't grabbed by the information they see here, they'll just zip by without ever reading your post.

Advertising Tip

The easiest and safest way to advertise your product or service in a newsgroup is to have someone else write the post for you in the form of an endorsement. In other words, if I wrote a post about one of my new books, it would be considered bragging and it would probably get me flamed. But if *you* wrote a post about one of my new books, it would be accepted and read with interest. Many times a post of this nature will begin, "I'm not getting anything to say this, but I read a great book the other day that I thought everyone here would like to know about." As long as the writer gives information, he or she is generally (but not always) safe.

After you've been online awhile, you'll develop friendships. Ask one of your friends to post a message about your product or service. This is not much different from asking someone for a

Figure 1-2

```
alt.business.misc (572T 666A OK OH R)              h=help

17  +       Seeking Global          DR Haz
            Business Contacts
18  +       Original Software       Gregory Yankelovic
            wanted
19  + 2     Invoice Purchasing      IPS
            Services
20  +       HOT STOCKS SPECIAL      Sheila Lotradu
            REPORT—LUMINART
21  +       Private Money Sources   Robert Sobel
22  +       ''Foreign Currency      Henry T Yaglowski
            Investing''
23  |       Make up to 50K in only  Steven Thompson
            60 Days ! ! ! !
24  +       *Accept Credit Cards*   MerchantAc
25  +       Quick cash, honest,     Internet CDS inCon
            legal money
26  +       Use your Computer to    !teven hompson
            earn up to 50K
27  +       #$%*>ONLINE             Linko
            MARKETING ALERT
            <*&%$#
28  +       5"×7" frames . . . 19   RogerMore
            cases left
29  +       Free CFRs on CD-ROM     Mark Wemhoff
30  + 7     800# UNLIMITED CALLS    Glen L. Roberts
            =>$19.95mo
31  + 2     $$$ Providing Drug      our libertarian
            Testing Help
32  +       Internet '95: Call for  rnet Presence(
            Submissions
```

testimonial. It's a safe form of indirect marketing, and it works online. (One word of caution: If the online readers sense that the testimonial is fabricated, you'll be flamed to death. Never post anything insincere.)

Here's one example of this method working well. When I was a member of an e-mailing list, someone asked whether there were any software programs available for helping with creativity. As it happens, one of my clients is Experience in Software, the creator of several programs for expanding creativity. I naturally posted the message shown in Figure 1–3. My client had several inquiries and orders as a result of my "ad." Again, testimonials work.

More Tips

1. *Do not post any ads unless you are in a group that accepts them.* The *biz.* groups may permit ads. So may some of the *alt.*

Figure 1-3

I use Thoughtline for writing. It helps me think through my project before I actually start scribbling. I also use Idea Generator Plus, a nifty and fun program for generating ideas. Not to be confused with the elaborate software called Idea Fisher, this one lets you role-play, create metaphors, answer questions, and so on. Very helpful, too.

For getting an overview of any project before attempting to solve anything, try Project KickStart. They say it will help you plan a direct route for success with any project within thirty minutes, and I'd agree.

All these programs are from Experience in Software. Call 1-800-678-7008 for a free catalog.

While I admit Experience in Software is my client and I write all the copy for its software, I'm not making a dime off this post. I just believe in what I'm suggesting. Still, I'd probably win a few points with the company if you called and said, ''Joe Vitale told me to call you. . . .''

Thank you.

groups. Other groups may allow ads if you add the word "AD" to the beginning or end of your headline. That way everyone knows your post is an advertisement. Again, read the posts for several weeks so that you have a feel for what is acceptable. Online advertising is becoming more and more common, but it is still not accepted across the board and may not be in this century. Post with care.

2. *Keep your posts short.* Restrict your posts to one paragraph. Your headline may have caught the attention of readers, but they are still busy and still eager to run on to other messages. Don't waste their time. Say what you have to say as succinctly as possible. One paragraph, or about seven lines of type, is a nice rule of thumb. Unless your post is riveting, few online readers will look beyond one screen of text per message. Keep that in mind as you write. Get to the point. Fast. If you have much more information, tell readers how to get it, by e-mailing you, calling, faxing, visiting your website, and so on. But as a rule of thumb, keep your newsgroup post down to a maximum of forty-eight lines or less.

3. *Use an engaging headline.* Your headline, called the "subject line" online, is the telegraphed message that attempts to stop prospects and urge them to read your post. When people log on and browse the Usenet group of their choice, all they see are headlines and authors' names. If your headline doesn't engage the reader, they will not read your post. Use a headline that sums up your message in the most intriguing way you can imagine. Ask yourself before posting, "Is this something these people will care about?"

4. *Give enough information.* Although you need to keep your messages short, you also need to give readers enough information so that they can make an informed decision whether to contact you or not for more details. Far too many online posts tease readers into responding. Their writers end up losing potential friends because they haven't said enough to amount to anything. Saying "E-mail for more details" won't work unless you've already given enough information in your post to generate sincere interest in your offer.

5. *Always end with a sig file.* Your signature file (which we'll discuss in a moment) promotes you and your business. Always

include it. It's an easy way to plug what you do while not appearing to hype yourself.

How to Start Your Own Newsgroup

It may seem that 10,000 groups are plenty, but there's a chance that you have a special interest or business that doesn't yet have a Usenet group. If that's the case, create your own. Again, scan all the groups and read the ones that are close to your area of interest. If there really isn't a group for your topic and you perceive a need for one, propose one. Here's how:

1. Select a name for your group.
2. Send your idea to *alt.config* with some reasons why this new group is needed.
3. Then, if your Usenet idea has been approved, send a message to *ccs@aber.ac.uk* asking for help in getting your group up and growing.
4. When your Usenet group is running, send a message announcing it to "Net Happenings" by sending e-mail to:

majordomo@is.internic.net.

5. Post a message in:

news.announce.newsgroups.

This is also a good place to ask for help in creating your own newsgroup.

Obviously, having your own group makes you king of the hill in that arena. It's another way to bring attention to you and your business.

Second Way: Identify Yourself With Sig Files

Readers don't know who you are. Text strips everyone of rank and status. A **sig file**, or signature file, is your opportunity to reveal who you are in a way that may bring you more business. Surprisingly, very few people use sig files online. Ending your post with "Mary Glenn" or "Nicholas Smith" conveys nothing. Unless you tell people who you are, they won't know. Unless you describe yourself, you're just another invisible creator of text. For that reason, be sure everything you post has a tightly written sig file at the end of it.

Your sig file doesn't need to be an advertisement. When I first started posting messages, I would add a fairly long sig file at the end of them. I would include my name, phone and fax numbers, and a list of my books as well as how to buy them. I quickly learned that was the wrong thing to do. Several people politely (and some not so politely) e-mailed me that my sig file was too long and too sales-oriented. I edited my signature.

Keep in mind that online readers want information. When they see your post, they aren't buyers. They are readers. You want to give them enough information so that they will want to contact you directly. When they do, you then have an opportunity to create a relationship with them, to tell them more about your products and services and, if all goes well, to turn them into buyers. As you'll discover, one of the fundamental truths of marketing is that people like to do business with people they know, like, and respect. Your sig file is an opportunity to begin that relationship.

Also, keep in mind that many readers have to pay for the messages they receive, and they often pay per line. If you had to pay for the junk mail you receive at home, would you like it? If your sig is over four lines, some people are bound to complain. Again, go for brevity.

Creating Sigs

Here are some guidelines for creating a sig file for yourself:

1. *Make it brief.* You're not posting a resumé. Just say who you are in the easiest and clearest terms. A rule of thumb in cyberspace is the shorter the sig file, the more important the person. It's easy to imagine that the President would simply say, "President, U.S.A." What else would be needed? If you have to spend paragraphs explaining who you are, you will be regarded

as an egotist desperately in need of attention. Four lines of text is generally considered safe.

2. *Give contact information.* Add your phone and fax numbers and always be sure to include your e-mail address. Although most online systems will automatically add your e-mail address to everything you post, don't count on it. Include your e-mail address so anyone can respond to you.

3. *Add a quote.* It's become customary to add a one- or two-line quote that sums up your philosophy of life or way of doing business. This quote is your opportunity to make people think, or smile, but certainly to remember you. A better line to add here is your "USP" (to be discussed in the next chapter).

Figure 1–4 shows two examples of effective sig files.

Third Way: Nothing but the FAQS

As mentioned earlier, FAQs are documents containing frequently asked questions. These files are extremely important, very popular, and nearly always read. Virtually every Usenet group and e-mailing list, many online businesses, and even some individuals have their own FAQ. It is a way to convey information simply, easily, and quickly. If it weren't for a FAQ, cyberspace would be jammed with people asking the same questions over and over (and over) again.

Figure 1-4

```
            College Aid Planning Strategies
New Video: ''Cash for College: Secrets to Getting Your
Fair Share''
e-mail: collgaid@hic.net

Joe ''Mister Fire!'' Vitale—e-mail: mrfire@blkbox.com
Author, ''The AMA Complete Guide to Small Business
Advertising''
See http://www.bookfair.com/publishers/awareness/
chap/
```

As you might guess, having a FAQ for you or your business can be highly valuable. When people ask you questions, refer them to your FAQ. When people want to know more about what you do, point to your FAQ. When you receive e-mail requests for your brochure, e-mail them your FAQ. You can even place your FAQ on a remote computer and allow people to download it whenever they want. It's a quick way of relaying information, and it's easy on you as well as your readers.

How to Write a FAQ

FAQs are easy to write if you keep in mind a few key points:

1. *Use the Q&A format.* FAQs rely on the tried-and-true question and answer format because that is the simplest way to get information across. If you or a Usenet group have been around for a while, you've heard the same questions asked numerous times. These are the questions to include in your FAQ. Naturally, your succinct answers are what you include, too.

2. *Be brief.* By now you know that everything you write online should be as brief and to the point as possible. There's simply too much happening online and too many other posts to read for anyone to spend a great deal of time on your material. Write a clear question and give a direct answer and move on to the next question. Ten lines of text seems like a wise target for each of your answers.

3. *Be lively.* FAQs that simply give "information" can be boring. Spice up your writing. Add eye-opening statistics, engaging stories, stimulating quotes. Make reading your FAQ a delight. Say something that surprises your readers. Add a fact that makes them sit up and say, "I didn't know that!"

4. *Give resources.* Although you aren't writing a term paper or dissertation, your FAQ is a resource for people. Make it a complete one by including details on how to get more information. If you have a list of books, articles, or tapes, include them. If you have a directory of people or places for people to contact for more information, include it. And remember to add your

own name, address, phone and fax numbers, and, of course, e-mail address.

5. *List questions up front.* It's common practice to list all the questions being answered in your FAQ at the beginning of the FAQ. This way anyone wanting to know the answer to a particular question can tell at a glance whether you cover it or not.

Sample FAQ Excerpt

There are well over 2,500 FAQs available. (If you're curious, you can retrieve them by a file transfer from *rtfm.mit.edu.* Just **ftp** [file transfer protocol] to *rtfm.mit.edu*; login *anonymous*; cd *pub/ Usenet/news.answers.* Or log on and browse the Usenet group, *news.answers,* a home for nearly all FAQs.) Figure 1–5 is an excerpt from a FAQ (complete with typos) to give you their look and feel.

Fourth Way: E-Mail and E-Mailing Lists Make Home Delivery Easy

Everyone online has an e-mail account. It's the most popular use of the online world. With it you can exchange e-mail with an estimated 50 million other users, including 20 million users who have e-mail access but don't have full Internet access. But there's another use for your e-mail account.

With e-mail you can subscribe to discussion groups of interest to you or your business. In other words, as you might subscribe to a magazine, you can subscribe online to mailing lists focused on particular topics. If you're interested in marketing online, you can subscribe to a mailing list called "Market-L." People post messages to that list relevant (we hope) to the subject of marketing. As the messages are posted, they are automatically sent by e-mail to everyone who subscribed to the list. Some lists have as few as a dozen subscribers; others may have hundreds or even thousands of people. You can never be sure because not everyone on the list participates in posting messages.

Subscribing to a list brings you up-to-the-minute (virtually, the second) news concerning the topic in question. I admit that a great many of the discussions on these lists seem like a waste

Figure 1-5

From Advertising on the Internet FAQ
by Michael Strangelove.
See http://www.phoenix.ca/sie for text.

''IS ADVERTISING ALLOWED ON THE INTERNET?''
   It is surprising how many people still see the
Internet as a noncommercial, academic, and technical
environment. Over 50 percent of the Internet is
populated by commercial users (that equals five to ten
million commercial users). The commercial Internet is
the fastest-growing part of cyberspace, which is
doubling in size every year. There are more business
users of the Internet than the total number of all the
users of all commercial networks combined.
   Over three years ago the U.S. National Science
Foundation lifted restrictions against commercial use
of the Internet's American backbone. Now an Internet
address on business cards is the latest craze. As the
Internet is not owned by any one company or nation, the
only real restrictions placed upon users are by the
consensus of the virtual community itself. The trick to
effective Internet advertising is taking the time to
learn what is and is not acceptable within any one of the
more than 7,000 online conferences.
   The one major exception to this is any Internet
users who have academic accounts provided by their
university or research institute. It is almost certain
that if you have an academic Internet account, you are
forbidden to engage in commercial activity over your
university's Internet connection. This may also hold
true for many FreeNets—if you are uncertain about local
authorized use policy, ask your Internet provider or
system postmaster. It should be noted that Usenet is no
less commercial than the rest of the Internet. Gone
forever are the days when the Internet was a private
club for the techno-elite.

of time; wait until you get dozens of e-mail messages from two people bickering with each other in public over a misspelled word. Still, being seen on the list can help you and your business. It's another form of marketing. Because I spent a few months as a subscriber to an e-mailing list developed by John Kremer on book marketing for publishers, I was seen by enough people on the list to be thought of as a book marketing expert. Several people bought my books, and a few have hired me to write press releases for them. By actively participating on the lists, I became known as someone you could trust.

But you can just as easily become known as someone who's a motormouth, windbag, or (and this is an online technical term) a bozo. Again, people judge you online by the text you send. That's all they have to go on. If you write material that isn't clear, isn't correct, isn't respectful, or isn't proofread, you may end up earning the reputation that you're not very professional. Before you post anything to an e-mailing list (or anywhere at all, for that matter), be sure you know how to write to communicate. Be sure you read and reread your message before sending it off for international exposure. The exposure you get may not be the exposure you want.

It was mentioned earlier, but it's worth repeating: People like to do business with people they know, trust, and respect. By participating in mailing-list discussions, you can position yourself as a reliable expert. The more you successfully "shmooze" online, the more you will be known. The more you are seen posting relevant commentary, the more you will be trusted. All this can lead to more business for you.

The Best Way to Post on E-Mailing Lists

Members of e-mailing lists are more sensitive to outright ads being posted than anyone else online. Some mailing lists will permit an advertisement if you add the word "AD" to the subject line of your post. (The FAQ for each mailing list will tell you what is acceptable.) Most lists won't tolerate any form of commercial message whatsoever.

The best way around all this is to think of how you would write to the editor of a major newspaper.

One day I wrote to *Inc.* magazine about an oversight in one of its articles. The magazine printed my letter, which just happened to include a line about what I do for a living. This was a legitimate way for me to get free advertising for my business. If I wrote a letter about my business and only about it, the letter would be crushed and trashed. It would be regarded as a blatant ad. But when I wrote a letter about something of concern to the magazine's readers, and mentioned what I do as an aside in the body of it, my message was accepted as a valid letter to the editor.

This works online as well. When you want to reply to something of discussion on the e-mailing list, find a way to work in a phrase that conveys the essence of your business. For example, a real estate broker once wrote to a mailing list to give her two cents about a recent hot issue. In her message she said, "As the owner of my own real estate firm in Houston, I've seen this issue surface many times, and here's what I think." Her carefully couched phrase successfully plugged her business. Anyone on the mailing list who sees her post, who lives in Houston, now knows whom to call for real estate sales. I've found this to be the safest and most effective way to "advertise" what you sell on an e-mailing list.

Where to Find E-Mailing Lists

There are over 11,000 e-mailing lists covering everything from aikido to zoology.

- For a catalog of lists, send e-mail to *mail-server@crvax.sri.com* with the message:

```
send interest-groups.txt
```

- For another catalog, send e-mail to *listserv@bitnic.bitnic* with the message:

```
list global
```

- You can also go directly to this website and browse 11,000 lists by aiming your pointer at **http://www.tile.net/**

listserv/ and letting *tile.net* automatically search for the mailing lists that would be the most beneficial for you to know about. Just type in the subject or key words and let *tile.net* do the rest. Impressive.

• Since no one site seems to have a complete catalog, you might also scan a directory of publicly accessible e-mailing lists at:

http://www.neosoft.com/internet/paml/

Subscribing to the lists is easy, but the process is different for each list. When you receive the above files of lists, you will also see the information on how to subscribe to each list. Most of the time you will send a message to a list server with an address such as *majordomo@world.std.com*. Usually the subject line will be left blank. Then, in your message, you will probably type the words "subscribe name-of-list" and that's it. Again, look at each list for directions on how to subscribe to it.

Useful E-Mailing Lists

To receive an e-mailing list for people interested in public relations, send e-mail as follows:

    To: majordomo@world.std.com
    Subject: [leave blank]
    Message: subscribe medialist

To subscribe to the *Market-L* list mentioned earlier, dedicated to the discussion of marketing, send e-mail as follows:

    To: listproc@mailer.fsu.edu
    Subject: [leave blank]
    Message: subscribe market-l your-name [replace
    ''your-name'' with your actual name]

Writing Help by E-Mail

Have a question about spelling, punctuation, or sentence structure? Purdue University has help for you. Just send an e-mail message with your question and within a few hours a real live professor will answer it. **OWL**, or the Online Writing Lab, is an e-mail-based information source from Purdue for questions related to writing. Send e-mail as follows:

```
To: owl@sage.cc.purdue.edu
Subject: owl-request
Message: send help
```

Transmit the message. You'll be sent complete information on how to use this service within fifteen seconds.

Explore the Entire Net by E-Mail

You can learn how to surf cyberspace and even conduct many full-access online functions with only an e-mail account. For complete details, request the remarkable information, "Doctor Bob's Guide to Offline Internet Access." Send e-mail as follows:

```
To: listserv@ubvm.cc.buffalo.edu
Subject: [leave blank]
Message: get internet by-mail nettrain f=mail
```

Fifth Way: HyperText—The Power of the Web

Despite the nervous-sounding name, hypertext is the wave of the online future. **Hypertext** is a way to create topic links in your writing. If this book were written in hypertext, whenever you saw a word in bold type, underlined, or in a different color, you could touch it and automatically be taken to a completely different page and begin reading text related to that word. This may sound confusing, but it's actually a way to enliven online text. Imagine reading a screen, coming across a word you didn't understand, and then clicking on it to learn all about the word. When you're through, press your back arrow key, and you're zipped back to the beginning page. That's hypertext.

The problem with hypertext is that writers of it can get out of hand. They often highlight too many words. That distracts from your reading. If I wrote this section in hypertext, I might highlight one important item per page as a way to link information. But I would not highlight every other word. Too many hypertext links makes readers stop and start too many times. It interrupts their natural reading. Imagine reading a pleasant novel but having to stop at every paragraph and go to your dictionary to look up the meaning of each new word, and you'll get a sense of the stop-and-start, jerky reading that too many hyperlinks can create.

Another problem with hypertext is that you can't use it in your e-mail or in any of your posts unless your reader has a special decoding program. Hypertext is designed for World Wide Websites (which we'll discuss in a moment). In other words, you can use it to write and design your own home page on the Web, and then let people know where it is so that they can visit it and read your text. But you can't e-mail your home page, complete with hypertext links, to anyone without it looking confusing.

Still, hypertext, properly used, is one of the most powerful forms of presentation around today. With it you can create online documents that not only look attractive, but can also include sights, sound, and even action. For the purposes of this book, we'll focus on using it to write even more effective online communications in what is called "The Web."

The World Wide Web

Imagine one million computers stationed around the planet. Then imagine that everyone who accesses those computers can design and leave available their very own documents, brochures, or greeting cards as a way to introduce themselves and what they do. In a real sense, cyberspace is like a spiderweb across the planet connecting computers by telephone wires and computer cables. This collage of unnumbered and unmapped computers makes up the World Wide Web, often called the Web or WWW. The documents themselves are called home pages or storefronts. These pages are made with hypertext.

There are several exciting reasons for using hypertext to design your own home page on the Web:

1. *Anyone can access it.* Once you've written and established your own home page, tell the world about it. Let everyone know that it's available by adding your home page's address, called an **URL** (a "Uniform Resource Locator," or online address, usually a lengthy series of letters and slashes, such as **http://www.fedworld.gov**) on everything you print and everything you post. When people visit your website, they'll learn more about you and what you do. (Look at one of my sites at **http://www.bookfair.com/publishers/awareness/amacom/**.)

2. *You can convey a whole lot of information.* As an example, I might create a home page that lists all my books. If you want information about any one title, you can click on that title and get transported to a page explaining what that book is about. If you want more information, there may be other links on the page that take you even deeper into my website. One of the links could even be arranged to take you to a website at another computer. The depth of any website, or the number of pages and links I can provide, is infinite. Think how much information you can convey when you have no limits!

3. *It's fun.* Websites are fun because they have so much richness. Your text and links alone can keep a reader busy for hours—and being able to add graphics, sound, and even multimedia can make your home page as fascinating as attending a carnival.

4. *It's good for business.* Many of your customers (potential and past) are using computers and online services to do business. Adding your home page to your marketing plans will win you extra points and lead to new business. This is why major-league players such as MCI, *Time,* and major newspapers have climbed aboard with their own websites.

If You Build It, Will They Come?

But be careful. Too many people are falling for the claim that having a website will bring millions of people to your business. Don't believe it.

Imagine a company saying, "We'll give you your very own

phone number and we'll list that number in our directory, and then we'll distribute that directory to millions of people."

Sounds exciting, doesn't it? That's what the phone company does: It gives you a phone number and lists it in all those phone books. But does that mean your phone will ring? No. You still have to promote your number and give people a reason to call before they ever will. A website is very much the same. Even if you have one, you still have to promote it through postings online, and through traditional channels, such as listing your URL (online address) in your ads, on your letterhead, and so on. So don't fall for the claim "If you build it, they will come."

Daniel Kehoe of Fortuity Consulting says, "Unless you dedicate yourself to an online promotional campaign, don't expect outstanding results. You need to post to newsgroups, mailing lists, and much more. If you don't tell people about your web pages, few will find them."

Warning: Malls Can Limp

Many enterprising individuals are creating malls online. These are WWW locations with more than one WWW business at them. They can be compared to shopping malls in large cities where there are several stores under one large roof. You visit an online mall by typing in its URL. When you get there you will see a directory of businesses. You can then click on any particular business, or roam the mall and visit all the businesses.

While this sounds like a logical way for your business to have a website and capture the attention of shoppers already gathered at one location, be careful. Some online malls fill their unlimited space with any business that will pay. Before you realize it, there are dozens of sites at the mall and too many for people to see without getting overwhelmed or bored. Your site gets lost in the crowd. In addition to that, the mall may permit competing businesses to remain at the mall. That could kill your sales.

A site called "Money Mall" (not its real name) is a good example. When the owner invited businesses to establish websites at his mall, his letter said, "Only one representative per company is allowed to be in my Money Mall." I quickly signed on, wrote sales copy to sell a product from a company I was affiliated with, and watched my website go online. Two months later, to my shock and dismay, I saw someone else at this mall selling the very same product from the very same company. When I protested, the owner said, "We allow the first person to use the company's name and logo. The next person can just talk about the product."

I read his original invitation letter back to him and he snapped, "You can read it and reread it all you want. This is our policy." The owner closed his ears to my pleas. He said, "You have to work with me on this." I was stunned and replied, "Me? I'm the customer. I'm paying you to work with me!"

He never did alter his policy. He, like many other online mall owners, was content to rake in money from unsuspecting business owners, not caring whether there were too many busi-nesses or competing businesses at his mall. He did not even care whether he honored his original word in his invitation letter.

Be careful of online malls. They may offer to write and de-sign a website for you, but make sure that (a) you will be the only business of your type at the mall, (b) the owner will at least promote the mall if not your site, and (c) the mall will limit its listings to no more than twelve businesses. Any more and browsers will become confused by all the choices. Any mall with that many businesses should open other malls, and break them into distinct categories.

Involve Your Users and Make Your Website Fun

While the WWW continues to receive all the latest hype, it's actually an overwhelming cybermonster full of advertisements. Some are calling the WWW "webertising" and "webcommer-cials."

Consider that there are over 4,000 books published every day around the world, many of them appearing as e-text . . . that television now has over 500 channels, some of which can appear online . . . that there are currently over 7,900 online databases . . . that there exists no definitive directory of websites because they are going up by the minute . . . that nearly all private or business websites are self-serving advertisements . . . consider all of that and you may have an inkling why web pages aren't the answer to easy sales online. There's simply too much information available in the world for any one site to get the attention it may deserve. And our information age just keeps getting bigger.

How do you get around this colossal mountain? How do you make your web page something someone will want to not only visit, but will revisit, will tell others about, and maybe even order something from? The answer lies in making your websites interactive and interesting. By "interactive" I don't mean keeping users busy clicking a mouse in an attempt to follow your hyperlinks. Instead, interactivity should be fun.

Take the Similarities Engine as an example. When you type in its website address, **http://www.ari.net/se/**, you're shot over to a page full of empty boxes. Fill out the top five boxes with the names of your five favorite music CDs and their artists. Then fill out the boxes for your name and e-mail address. Now send it off. Within one to three days you will receive an e-mail message back containing the Similarities Engine's suggestions on other CDs and artists that you may also enjoy.

Not only does this website involve the user, it also encourages him or her to buy more CDs. After I entered my five top CDs, I received a message listing eighty-three other CDs that I might like, based on the type of music the computer figured made my blood dance. I printed out the list and went to a music store, and now I own more CDs than I need. All because of a website that was interactive and interesting. I've also told others about this website, including you, because the site is fun. Make your own web pages fun and interactive and you may have similar results.

Writing Hypertext

Since this not a technical book, I will not explain how to design your own hypertext documents. But I can offer some suggestions to keep in mind when you hire a technical person to help you, or when you use a software program to create one yourself.

1. *Don't overdo the links.* As I mentioned earlier, one hyperlink per screen of text is probably plenty. Any more than that

and you risk confusing people . . . or even yourself. Keeping up with all the links can be a nightmare. Too many make reading difficult.

2. *Don't overdo the graphics.* Not everyone can see graphics online. Even those who can usually don't have the patience to download large graphic files. If users have slow modems, waiting for a graphic to appear on their screens might take several minutes . . . time for which they are being charged for by their access provider or long-distance phone company. Use graphics sparingly.

3. *Remember, text rules in cyberspace.* Don't get fancy with graphics or hypertext links. Ease of communication and clarity of use should be your targets. Always aim for simplicity. If your copywriting isn't compelling, few will buy. True, online browsers certainly want information, but don't feed it to them in dry chunks. The more you can add emotional excitement to your words, the better your chances of being read, being remembered, and having your services bought.

4. *Be interesting.* Vary what you write. Some people create their own paperless documents, such as e-zines, or electronic magazines, and design them for home page use. There are far too many diversions for readers in cyberspace, so don't bore anybody. With one click they can leave your site and never return. Keep what you say interesting. Always think of your readers and give them what they want, not what you want. My rule of thumb in writing any marketing piece is, "Get out of your ego and into the reader's ego." Write what would keep them interested. As Howard Gossage, a famous ad man, once said, "People read whatever interests them, and sometimes it's an ad." Make your online text interesting and they just might read what you write. Vary your site every day (yes, every day) and browsers just might return again to see what's new.

5. *Include contact information.* Be sure you place your name, address, phone, fax, and e-mail address on every page of your website documents. You never know when a reader will suddenly want to contact you. Don't make that person backtrack through several layers of hyperlinks just to find out your phone number. Put your contact information at the top of every page.

WWW Sites to Visit

http://www.ids.net/~rebecca/index   The above website contains lists and links to numerous writing-related resources.

http://www.bookfair.com/publishers/awareness/amaweb/   This URL will bring you to a website describing one of my earlier books, *The Seven Lost Secrets of Success*. Note: This is also an example of a shameless plug for one of my earlier books. If I posted something like this online, I would probably be flamed.

http://www.bookfair.com/welcome/cyberwriter/new   The Copywriting Profit Center at that URL contains excerpts from this book, updated information on how to market your business online, and many impressive links to other profit-generating sites.

http://www.experienceware.com   Check out Project Kickstart, a software program to help you set up an Internet marketing strategy. That and more are at that site.

http://www.newmarket-forum.com/assoc.html   This site lists more than 10,000 professional associations and membership groups, searchable by name, address, and phone number.

http://www.sbaonline.sba.gov   You'll find the U.S. Small Business Administration at that address.

http://arganet.tenagra.com/Tenagra/net-acceptable.html   There you'll discover helpful information on acceptable online marketing and advertising.

http://www.charm.net/~windsor/todayad.html   Tim Windsor is a copywriter who spends a lot of time online searching for cyberads (both good and bad) worth studying. You can follow his path here.

http://www.yahoo.com/   Probably the most popular site on the WWW. Yahoo is a monster online catalog containing well over 50,000 links to other websites. It is a "search engine" that you can use to locate specific information at other websites.

http://www.altavista.digital.com   Will let you search Usenet groups as well as websites across cyberspace.

http://www.lycos.com   This monster catalog zips through over 60 million links in seconds to search for whatever you want.

http://www.cs.colostate.edu/~dreiling/smartform.html   This is the most powerful search engine I know of because it automatically searches up to fifteen major Internet catalogs, including Yahoo, for the data you ask it to locate.

http://www.tig.com/IBC/   This Internet Business Center site about the online business world contains impressive information, statistics, news, and links to other sources.

http://www.homecom.com/global/pointers.html   Once you have your own website, you can have it automatically linked to several other popular websites, at no charge, by completing the form at the above address.

Note: If the URL for any site has changed (this happens a lot in cyberspace), you can always perform a key word search at Lycos or Yahoo to find the new URL.

Summary

I don't know whether Michael Wolff, the flamed author we talked about at the beginning of this chapter, wrote newsworthy posts or sales-oriented ones. It's difficult to say since his posts were deleted by "Cancelmoose."

However, the above five basic ways for capturing attention on the e-frontier will work for you if you carefully follow the guidelines and learn how to write to sell (which is where we're going next in this book).

Remember, cybertravellers want news above all else. Feed them exciting news items and relevant information, and the chances of your messages being erased are greatly diminished. In short, give online readers what they want and watch them come to you with their business. As Zig Ziglar has said, "You can get whatever you want if you help enough people get what they want."

Now let's get more specific.

2

What Is Your "USP"?

Online or not, most people have no idea what they are selling or to whom they are trying to sell it. A common mistake is thinking "my product or service is for everybody." That's why many people jump online, in the hope of reaching the alleged millions of people surfing cyberspace. But the reality is that the tighter your focus, the better your results.

Advertising man David Marinaccio wrote a terrific book entitled *All I Really Need to Know I Learned From Watching Star Trek*. One of his points I liked best was the idea that everyone on board the Starship Enterprise knows the ship's purpose. Ask the dumbest ensign, "What's your mission?" and you'll get the famous opening line from the television series. But ask people in an average business what their mission is and they'll look at you as if you spoke Klingon. Clearly, knowing your mission helps direct your flight through space . . . even cyberspace.

But does it help sell anything?

How to Make Money Online

If your intention is to make money online (or anywhere else), a mission statement alone isn't enough. A mission statement can act as a flight plan, but it lacks persuasion. For that, you also need to know your "USP," or unique selling proposition. Your USP will help you find your niche, and your niche is where you'll find your pot of gold.

Although many marketing gurus today talk about a USP, the concept itself is several decades old. The late Rosser Reeves, author of *Reality in Advertising*, developed the idea of a USP back in the 1940s. In short, a USP declares your difference in the marketplace. It's a one-line statement (proposition) that explains what is different (unique) about what you are offering (selling). Your USP becomes your "copy logo," the phrase that separates you from the crowd in a way your prospects remember. Knowing your USP helps you focus on your service and your market; broadcasting your USP helps you nail the people who want your services.

Examples of USPs

- Amazon Books' USP can't be beat: "The world's largest online bookstore."
- Domino's has a USP that created a pizza empire: "Fresh, hot pizza delivered to your door in 30 minutes or less, guaranteed."
- In a world focused on hot tea, Luzianne "iced tea bags" is a USP.
- So is "mountain grown" coffee.
- So is "soap that won't dry your hands like ordinary soap."
- M&M candies created the USP "melts in your mouth, not in your hand."
- When it comes to helping people become authors, my own USP is "I'm the only man to help you write, publish, and market your books."
- As a direct mail copywriter I use this USP: "Inventor of the Hot-Button Headline and Hypnotic Sales Copy." Now that I'm in cyberspace, my new USP has become "The World's First CyberCopywriter."

How to Create a USP

Your USP defines your place in the marketplace in a way that makes you distinct from . . . and better than . . . everyone else. Here are some questions to help you figure out your own USP:

1. *What are you selling?* Write down what you think your product or service is. This can be as obvious as "We sell car-

pets," or you can add something that your service provides: "We sell carpets that make your feet feel better and your home look more attractive."

2. *What is unique about what you sell . . . or how you sell it?* You have competitors. What separates you from them? What do you offer that they don't? What is unique about you? Or what can you make unique about your business? Write down your answers.

3. *How can you describe both answers in one tight, persuasive line?* This may take some work. Write as many one-line statements as you can generate. The more you have, the better. Afterward, tinker with them, combine them, and see whether you can come up with a one-line statement that declares your uniqueness. That will be the beginning of your USP.

Be careful of using empty words such as "quality" and "service" or "the best." Saying you sell furniture of the highest quality means nothing. What exactly does "quality" mean? Do you use a particular brand of wood? Say so. Saying you deliver "outstanding service" also means little. How is your service great? Do you answer the phone on the second ring, make house calls, stay open Sundays, give away puppies? Say so.

Tips From the Master

Rosser Reeves offered several suggestions on how to write your own USP in his classic book, *Reality in Advertising*. Here are three of them:

1. *"Each advertisement must make a proposition to the consumer."* Your USP should describe exactly what someone will get from buying your product or service. What is the benefit from people doing business with you? Online or not, knowing what your business helps "cure" will help you describe and position yourself in the marketplace. What is your proposition?

2. *"The proposition must be one that the competition either cannot, or does not, offer."* What is unique about your business? You

must stand out from the crowd if you want prospects to come to you. How are you different from your competitors? What do you do that they don't?

3. *"The proposition must be so strong that it can move the mass millions."* You might be able to write a sentence that states a proposition, and even a unique one, but unless it persuades people to do business with you, it's incomplete. Your USP has to have persuasive power. It needs to state a reason for people to spend their money with you. Why should anyone give you money for your service?

Writing a sentence that satisfies all three of Reeves's points will help you create an unforgettable USP. As Reeves pointed out, very few businesses have a clue about their USP. Write one that makes you and your business shine and you will stand out online (and off) as a power to reckon with.

Look Deep

A young man came to me one day wanting to market himself as a speaker. He was already online but wasn't sure how to begin advertising himself there. The first thing I did was sit him down and ask him a direct question, "How are you different from all the other speakers in the world?"

"I motivate people to set goals and attain them," he began. I stopped him and pointed out that there is no shortage of motivational speakers. How was he different from the rest? He then said he was more spiritually based in his approach. "That's getting closer to it," I said, "but we still haven't found what makes you unique."

"Well, I used to play the guitar and harmonica and perform," he replied. "I want to be the first speaker to use the theater to help people change and go for their dreams."

There it was. His uniqueness was in what he brought to his career from his past. By claiming that he was a motivational speaker who entertained his audience while educating them, he developed a USP that helped separate him from the herd. I urged him to work on that unique angle until he could state it

in one line, and then to use that USP as his touchstone throughout his online marketing.

How to Test Your USP

How do you know whether your USP will work?

An attorney told me his USP was "I help injured victims in
their quest for justice." He wanted to know whether it was good.
I asked one question: "Can any other attorney say the same
thing?" He said yes. I said, "Then your USP isn't good enough."

Ask yourself whether your competitors can use your USP.
If they can, then you haven't written yours to reveal your
uniqueness. What is different about your service? How do you
differ from your competitors? What can you do that they can't,
or haven't, done yet?

Make your USP yours and yours alone.

Sig Tip

One of the best uses for your USP is adding it to your sig file.
Rather than adding a one-line quote from a celebrity, or a humorous remark, add your USP. Let it stand as a brief introduction to you and your service. This is a very effective and
flameproof way to communicate what you do whenever you
post something online.

You Can Be the First

Despite what I just said about the importance of uniqueness,
keep in mind that sometimes the only thing different between
you and your competitors is being the first to state the obvious.

When Claude Hopkins, arguably the greatest copywriter of
all time, had to sell Van Camp's pork and beans in the early
1900s, he couldn't find anything unique about them. He decided
to tell facts the competitors never told. He said the beans "were
grown on special soils." All navy beans were. Hopkins was sim-

ply the first to say so, and that created a powerful USP. Anybody who said the same thing afterward would be viewed as imitating the king of beans.

There may be other cybercopywriters online, but I'm the first to claim that distinction. For that reason alone, it makes a memorable USP for me. I've preempted the competition simply by declaring my position in the marketplace. You can do the same thing. Just stake out your territory.

Your USP can act as a one-line advertising message. Make it short, clear, and direct, and you can run it in your online ads, focus all your marketing on promoting it, print it on the back of your business cards, add it to your signature file, and keep it in the front of your prospects' minds at all times.

Summary

Your USP may seem tight and restrictive to you. If so, great! That means you have found your niche. You have cornered your share of the market. And like the Starship Enterprise, you'll find that your niche contains unexplored regions . . . and your USP will keep you on the right "trek" to unfathomed profits in the exciting world of cyberspace.

3

The New Way to CyberWrite a Persuasive E-Sales Letter

Writing a sales letter for any audience and any medium is tough work. That's why some of the best copywriters are paid up to $25,000 to compose just one persuasive letter. But writing sales letters online, or e-letters, has its own set of benefits and challenges.

On the one hand, there are no postal costs. A letter you mail via "snail mail," or through the regular U.S. Postal Service, will cost you anywhere from 8.3 to 32 cents each. And that's if you mail only in the States. Overseas mail costs even more. But mailing costs online are zip. It doesn't cost you a dime to send one letter or even several thousand letters. That's good.

On the other hand, you're writing for a completely new medium. Traditional sales letters can use a variety of cosmetic devices, from all caps to handwritten comments or underlining, to make the letter more readable. Not so online. Electronic text can appear only in a certain format, because there are over 50,000,000 possible readers of it who are using a staggering variety of different computers and different software. Some people might be able to see a graphic in your letter. Most will see only a set of very strange letters and marks that have no meaning. Those symbols are not very persuasive.

There's another issue: To whom can you send e-letters? Out in the real world you can rent mailing lists of people who may be interested in your product or service and send them all your sales letter. They may call it junk mail, but if it works, you'll call it easy money. But online you cannot easily send unsolicited e-mail. Try it and you may quickly get bombarded with hate mail. You may also get, as one small business found out, death threats. Any way you look at it, that's bad public relations.

What do you do? How do you write an e-sales letter that not only gets accepted online, but gets you the results you want?

Step One: Post a Sign

Your e-sales letters will be received with an open mind if they are requested. How do you get people to actually ask for your sales materials? It's easier than you might think. In mail order it's called "the two-step." Here's how it works:

Newsgroups

The easiest and fastest thing to do is post an intriguing or informative message about your product or service in the appropriate newsgroup.

As we already noted, there are over (at last count) 10,000 newsgroups on Usenet, which is available to virtually every cyberspace traveller. Most of these groups are very active and well-read information centers. No matter what you are offering, there's probably a group for you. The most obvious newsgroups for a business message are titled *biz.misc* and *alt.business.misc*. Any group beginning with *biz.* would be a good bet. But searching through all the groups will turn up the right ones for your product or service.

Next, post a message in the appropriate group or groups. This message needs to be very short and to the point. You'll need a headline, because the newsgroups are listed by subject line only. Readers will decide to read or pass up your post from your headline, so make it a grabber. I strongly advise against tricking people. I once saw a header that said, "FREE SEX WITH SHARON STONE!" I immediately hit my enter key so I could see the ad, and was depressed to see that it was a bait for a long-distance telephone service. Even if I had been interested in the service, the way I was swindled into reading the ad would have left me in a sour mood. Don't trick your potential customers. They'll resent it. Even if they do somehow remember you and your headline, they will remember it in a negative way. No business can afford to have that type of negative PR.

Some of the worst writing in cyberspace is the headlines for the newsgroups' posts. Headlines are supposed to snare the people who would be most interested in your product or service. That rarely happens online. Figure 3–1 is an example of a screen from the newsgroup called *alt.business.multi-level*, for people interested in network marketing opportunities. None of those headlines grab me. Yet if you aren't hooked by the headline, you'll never read what the post under the headline has to say.

Figure 3–2 shows another screen, this one from the *misc.entrepreneurs* group, for would-be or practicing entrepreneurs. There are a few interesting headlines here, but not many. That's one of the first problems people have writing online. They don't create a compelling headline. Most online users compose their messages on the fly, while sitting in front of their computer and without much previous thought. It's far wiser to spend some time offline writing headlines, thinking about them, and then posting the most riveting one online. This way your headline will leap off the screen because of its strength.

An example of a smart headline that works is this one from Sheila Danzig:

TURN ANY COMPUTER INTO A MONEY MACHINE!

Everyone reading it is sitting at a computer, and since the headline is posted in a business section, everyone there is looking for ways to make money. When you choose to see what this headline is all about, you get the following post:

Millionairess Reveals Amazing Secret. FREE REPORT
Call 305–425–7564 Operator SMPL (24 hours)
Or send e-mail to CompuServe: 72210,141

Obviously, when people respond to her ad, they end up receiving her e-sales letter. This is an example of a headline and

Figure 3-1

```
alt.business.multilevel (248T 427A OK OH R)     h=help

 1   +     Behind the Disguise      Bill Ataras
           (The Amway Phenomenon)
 2   + 7   Jester, AMWAY, the       Bill Ataras
           System
 3   +     Dental                   Charles Wohlberg
           Breakthrough!!!
 4   +     Don't Tell Anyone        Jeff Freeman
 5   + 2   Common Wealth            Jeff Freeman
           Scholastic
           Corporation
 6   +     tonison@aol.com          Mickatavage
           should be blacklisted
 7   + 2   Fire Your Boss!          michaelj@crocker.c
 8   +     Business Opportunity     michaelj@crocker.c
 9   +     Amway buy-back           Jim LaCroix
           guarantee
10   + 2   PHIL—Seeking Amway       Jim LaCroix
           Dist. The System
11   + 2   HERBALIFE                Gumby
12   + 2   ADMIN FEE                ARTHUR BOUCHARD
           DISCLOSURES??
13   +     Ginseng Products ready   Tom Twitty
           to market
14   +24   TPN (The Peoples         Charlo Barbosa
           Network)
15   + 8   Excel's Position in      Ken Leonard
           Market
16   + 5   Is anyone making any     Dale Windle
           money?
```

Figure 3-2

```
misc.entrepreneurs (400T 474A OK OH R)          h=help

  1  + 2   Business Opportunity   pc-1000
           In The Vinyl Sign
           Business
  2  +     Money From Home        pc-1000
  3  +     LOW-COST advertising/  Paul Ganade
           PR for small biz
  4  +     *** LOTTO NEWS ITEMS IN  Paul Ganade
           REC.GAMBLING
  5  +     Professionals          Paul Ganade
           Networking
  6  +     900 ADULT LINES CAN    Jim LaCroix
           MAKE YOU THOUSANDS!!
  7  + 2   CHINA BUSINESS JL.     Wei Shyu
           50213 Contents List
  8  + 4   Reverse Phone Book on  jasmine
           CDROM? Where Buy
  9  +     Huge excess OEM        Chuck Moore
           electronics parts for
           sale
 10  +     QUICK CASH! <snicker>  Stuart Whitmore
 11  + 2   Does anyone do         Paul Saucier
           international
           receivables
 12  +     Interactive Training   ChrisMerrick
           Software
 13  +     WANTED:MANUFACTURERS   Cindy Roberts
           OF ADULT TOYS
 14  +     home business          Bobby Shea
 15  +     Business plan writing  Mac or Doug Geiste
           software for
 16  +     New Satellite Network: Bob Beck
           The Peoples Network
```

a post that work. Both are short, direct, and relevant to the people looking at them on that business newsgroup. (It's important to note that this style of headline and post will *not* work on most other groups. It is too heavy-handed and sales-oriented. But in the business groups, this style works.)

So the first way to get people to read your e-writings is to create headlines that generate interest, and then post them in the appropriate newsgroups.

Mailing Lists

The other way to encourage people to contact you is by posting a news message on the appropriate mailing list.

Again, there are over 11,000 mailing lists covering everything from acupuncture to zippers. Find the list that is the most natural fit for your product or service. There are also business and marketing and "what's new" mailing lists available. People interested in the subject of the list subscribe to it. While most readers just read their mail, many of them post items of interest, opinions, and such on the mailing list. Then, either daily or weekly, everyone on the list receives the postings. All you have to do is post a news- or opinion-oriented message about your product or service and invite people to write to you for more details.

For example, when I was first experimenting with marketing in cyberspace, I enlisted the help of Cliff Kurtzman, President of Tenagra, an Internet marketing company, to help me post a message on the marketing mailing list. Cliff composed a friendly, low-key memo for me that said I was doing research on cyberspace marketing and had some columns available if anyone wanted to see them. All you had to do was send e-mail to me to have the columns sent.

This was clearly an acceptable way to get leads of people interested in receiving my e-letter. The people reading the mailing list were interested in marketing, and we offered them marketing information (my columns). Like most cybertravellers, these people wanted information, so we offered it to them and said they could get more by e-mailing me. Within a few days over 150 people from thirteen countries requested more information. When people wrote, they received my disguised e-letter (which you'll get to read in a moment).

You still need a headline to use this approach, because when people receive their e-mail, they will see a subject line that describes (we hope) the message. I often receive up to 100 messages a day. I use the subject line to decide whether I want to read the message or just delete it. Your readers will do the same. Make sure your subject line becomes an enticing headline.

All the posts will be e-mailed to everyone who subscribes to the mailing list. But you can't offer fluff, and you can't try to sell anything directly unless you place the word "AD" at the beginning or end of your subject line. Instead, you would be better off posting opinions or asking questions about products or services that relate to your business. In this way you establish yourself as an authority in your field, and you gain rapport with the rest of the readers on the mailing list. In addition, every time you post a message, you are promoting yourself and your business.

Figure 3–3 is an example of a post to an Internet marketing mailing list, placed by Herman Holtz. His on post is low-key and sincere. He isn't trying to sell himself, yet notice that the post's very existence helps establish him as an authority. And notice that the post ends with a "signature," a short bio that softly plugs Holtz's books.

Also notice that although Holtz is an author with dozens of books in print, his post is not well written. There are several strange phrases in it. Look at the statement in his first point, "The *perception* is more important than the reality, of course." What does that mean? And earlier he wrote, "Must what is offered be truly unique?" That, too, is awkward. This is the type of writing you'll find online, and it's not very persuasive.

I am a fan of Holtz's work, but think he could have done better in this case.

Subject Lines That Get Noticed

Again, the first thing people will see is your subject line, and that has to serve as a powerful headline or you've lost people right there. Think of what would interest your readers. If

Figure 3-3

Date: Tue, 17 Jan 1995 14:15:55 -0800
From: Herman Holtz <holtz@clark.net>
To: inet-marketing@einet.net
Subject: Re: INET-MARKETING digest 189
Message-ID: <v02110174ab41f143c4a2@[204.94.44.2]>
    I think the notion expressed here quite often that
we must teach the consumer new habits and new attitudes
is a hazardous one. People in general resist change, and
they especially resist revolutionary change. Change
they must, but they must not recognize that change is
being forced upon them. They must be reassured by seeing
familiar ideas and methods.
    I doubt that online marketing—and it is online
marketing, not Internet marketing—has much
correspondence with malls and retail outlets, so I have
misgivings about trying to make shoppers perceive
online marketing in that mode. On the other hand, mail
order/direct mail marketing is now so well established
that there is little about it that is foreign to any
buyer. I see online marketing as much more akin to mail
order and direct mail marketing, and I would suggest
using the truths and methods of that field as the line of
departure here.
    The question has been raised as to why a buyer would
shop online for what he or she could buy in some nearby
retail store. Excellent point, and we can turn to mail
order again in seeking an answer. One thing that helps a
mail order venture success is being able to offer
something not normally available in the classic
markets—the unique selling proposition, in fact.
    I think that is one reason bookstores are likely to
do well. Ordinary bookstores—even superstores, such as
Borders—do not do the greatest job of maintaining
inventory. Again and again, the online bookstore can
ship a book that you cannot find on the shelves at Borders
or SuperCrown.
    But what is a ''USP''? Must what is offered be truly

(continues)

Figure 3-3 (continued)

> unique? Must it somehow be different enough to be
> obtainable nowhere else? No, that is, in fact not
> necessary for at least two reasons:
>   1. The *appearance* of being unique or radically
> different is enough. The *perception* is more
> important than the reality, of course. One needs some
> creative copy—some imagination in presentation.
>   2. If the product or service is not unique, perhaps
> the offer may be unique in some other way: Price?
> Packaging? Guarantee? Other?
>   * * *
>
> Herman Holtz [holtz@clark.net]: Independent
> Marketing Consultant, Writing and Ghostwriting
> Services. Author of 60+ books, including best-selling
> ''How to Succeed as an Independent Consultant''. P.O.
> Box 1731, Wheaton, MD 20915. 301-649-2499. Fax: 301-
> 649-5745.

you come across as too sales-oriented, you will be ignored or flamed. If your headline is vague, few people will choose to read your message.

Your safest bet is going for a straight benefit headline. In other words, if you are a chef, maybe your post can have the heading "Pleasing holiday crowds with pasta." If you're a computer programmer with a new software package, you might post something in a computer newsgroup that says, "This new software solves impotency." (Of course, if your software doesn't cure impotency, don't say it does.) Clearly focus on the benefits to the reader. The more you can write a subject line that intrigues your prospects in a relevant way, the more people will make the choice to read your post.

A few more suggestions:

1. *Use your USP.* How does your service differ from your competition's? Make that the focus of your subject. If you are offering something new, say so. "New" grabs attention.

2. *Be specific.* Don't use vague words or tease people with empty phrases. Say exactly what your post is about. "The best" means nothing; "Rated #1 by . . ." creates credibility and interest.

3. *Use emotional words.* Rather than saying, "Protect yourself," say "Save your neck." Make your headline seem alive by using emotionally rich phrases.

4. *Be relevant.* Be sure you post your message in the group(s) that would care about it. Posting a message about your financial services in a group discussing movies would get you flamed.

Posts That Get Results

Your actual message has to be short, direct, and appealing—and yet give enough information for people to want to read more. (See Chapter 7 on how to write an e-ad for a complete description on how to write a message that gets results.) Keep in mind that your message can't seem like an ad. It has to read like interesting news from an intelligent friend. In other words, pretend you are writing your message to one person. Say what you need to say, in a way that would interest that person, and shut up.

Think of how you communicate with a friend or colleague when you discover a new restaurant, book, or movie that you like. You don't call your friends and "sell" them on it. You simply talk to them about the experience and invite them to try the food, the book, or the movie for themselves. That's the spirit your post needs to have. Tell people just enough to make them want more, and end by saying that if they call, fax, or e-mail back, they will get a special report (your disguised sales letter) explaining the whole thing.

Step Two: The E-Sales Letter

Before I tell you how to write a special report, or disguised sales letter, let me say that you can probably take any sales letter and adapt it for e-use in the appropriate business group. Note that I said business group. Trying to post a traditional sales letter, even adapted for e-use, could get you flamed in other groups.

Still, if you don't make some fundamental changes to your sales letter, your winning letter will get *zero* response in any business group and could even get you kicked off your Internet provider's service. For safety's sake, read and memorize the following tips:

1. *Rarely use ALL CAPS.* All caps in a real-world letter simply mean you are stressing a point. But online, all caps mean you are YELLING. They have a very negative, even angry connotation. When you want to stress a word, put asterisks around it, like this: *yelling*. While you will often find all caps in e-messages, they are not recommended.

2. *Keep your margins wide.* You can use narrow margins on regular letters, but online your wide sentences may not get seen, or they may get reproduced in an irregular format. It'll be very tough to read. E-sales letters need to have margins set at 20 and 80, so every sentence is very short and will get displayed on any screen, even if it's a laptop, without odd text breaks. My own rule of thumb is to keep text down to 60 characters wide. As I'm typing, I'm looking at the screen. When the lines look as if they are beyond four inches, I hit my return key to force a carriage return. This way all my posts are narrow enough to be read by virtually everyone online without difficulty.

3. *Don't use graphics.* As mentioned earlier, you can't use graphics in e-mail. Most computer users don't have the capability to read anything but ASCII format, or straight text. Trying to add drawings, even ones made by ASCII characters that "should" be readable by everyone, isn't worth the risk.

4. *Information is the gold in cyberspace.* Trying to sell readers with a traditional hyped-up sales letter won't work. People online want information and lots of it. You'll have to add solid material to your puffed-up sales letter to make it work online. Refrain from saying your service is "the best" or that you offer "quality." Those are empty, meaningless phrases. Be specific. How are you the best? What exactly do you mean by quality? And who says it besides you? And even though I say that infor-

mation is the gold, readers don't want to be bored. They seek, like all of us, excitement. Give it to them.

5. *Online letters can be far longer than other letters.* Again, cybertravellers want information. As long as you are giving them interesting information, they'll keep reading. You know this from your own experience. You'll read whatever interests you, even if it is book-length. As soon as you lose interest, you stop. People online are the same. Make your posts interesting. Ask yourself before posting anything, "Will my readers be glad I sent them this?"

6. *Avoid emoticons.* Because you can't express emotions such as humor, surprise or sarcasm in ASCII text, online users have developed symbols conveying those messages. These icons are called "smileys" or "emoticons." For example, :) means "happy face." (Tilt your head to the left and look at the symbol. See the smile?) : -0 means surprise; : - < means sad. While many online travellers are familiar with these "communicons" (communication icons), many of them don't understand what the symbols mean. I suggest that you rarely use them in an e-sales letter. Knowing about them will help you read online text, but using them may confuse some of your potential readers.

In addition, remember that online readers are extremely resistant to blatant ads. There are even software programs available that will block sales letters from being read! (Remember "Cancelmoose"?) These programs are the equivalent of blocks on your phone to prevent unwanted telephone solicitation, or locks on your cable television to prevent access to certain stations.

So how do you get around all this in the e-world?

The Disguised E-Sales Letter

You can send a "special report" to prospects that is nothing more than a disguised sales letter, or at least a less obvious one.

What exactly does that mean?

Earlier I mentioned that Cliff Kurtzman helped me post a message on a mailing list about my researching Internet marketing. When people expressed interest in what I was doing, I sent them one of my columns. My columns had previously been printed in a major magazine and were all rich in information, but they were also sales tools. In other words, every column softly plugged me, my services, or my books. This format doesn't hit readers as hard as a traditional sales letter, but it's more acceptable and far easier to read online. Readers on mailing lists and in more conservative newsgroups want *information*.

Let me give you an example. Figure 3–4 shows one of my more popular columns and one Cliff and I made available online. The column isn't as punchy as the type of letter you might find in your mailbox at home or work, but it's still smooth, interesting, and sales-oriented. Its format is more appropriate for online selling because it focuses on information. This is the type of letter that you can safely post or e-mail. Let me explain:

1. *Notice the riveting headline.* Once again, you want to entice people to keep reading. This headline holds a major promise. It's difficult to pass up reading the column after seeing this headline. When this column was posted on CompuServe (see GO WORK on CompuServe to find my columns in its online library), over 600 people saw the headline and then read the column. Another column of mine posted on CompuServe, titled "How to Write a Million-Dollar Sales Letter!" was read by nearly 300 people within twenty-four hours. Powerful headlines pull in readers.

2. *Notice that the column offers concrete examples.* While those stories illustrate the message I am giving, they also sell. I mention several of my books in the column, and don't say I'm selling them at all. But I've written about them in such a way that people become naturally eager to have them. People from around the world saw the books mentioned and e-mailed me about ordering them. One of the people who ordered my self-published book, *Hypnotic Writing*, became the next publisher for that very book.

3. *Notice that I offer something free.* This is a technique that works just about anywhere. But one of the reasons I wrote this column was to repay a favor to John Martin, the publicist mentioned in the piece. This worked. John received over 150 requests

Figure 3-4

From: mrfire@blkbox.com
Joe Vitale 713-999-1313
Box 300792, Houston 77230

How to Make Business Stampede to Your Door This Year by Joe Vitale

How would you like to start the new year by getting 30,000 phone calls from prospects eager to do business with you?

It's easier than you think. My hope is that the new year will be one in which all those in business begin to help themselves by helping the media. Let me explain:

When I wrote and self-published ''Hypnotic Writing,'' my manual on copywriting, I bought the mailing list of all the writing magazines in the country. I sent a one-page news release to each. One day I opened up one of the national magazines, and there was a half-page article about my book! It was my entire news release! Had I paid for the advertising, it would have cost me a few hundred if not thousand dollars. As it was, the exposure cost me about thirty cents.

My best-seller is ''Turbocharge Your Writing.'' I figured the readers of ''Target Marketing'' would be interested because many marketing people rely on the formula in the book to write their sales letters, so I sent a news release to them. The editor called and said, ''Are you prepared to handle about two hundred calls?'' I said sure. Then I persuaded him to list my address in the magazine, rather than my number, as a service to his readers. All they would have to do is send me a check for the book. I'm still getting orders!

One of my clients is a real estate broker. We sent a news release out about his service and his new book. ''Woman's Day'' magazine called him and wanted to buy the rights to excerpt an article from his book. We agreed, as long as they gave him a resource box explaining how readers could contact the author. The

(continues)

Figure 3-4 (continued)

editor said, ''Are you prepared to handle thirty to
forty thousand phone calls?'' We'll handle it, we said.

When I was promoting the autograph party for my
latest book, ''The AMA Complete Guide to Small Business
Advertising,'' I created a simple contest where the top
three most unusual business ideas would receive free
copies of the book. I wrote a release and sent it out.
The ''Houston Post'' ran it on the front page of its
business section!

The press is powerful. When Sharon Holmlund's
business was mentioned in ''Home Office Computing''
magazine, she received over 400 inquiries. When Sharon
Olson received a plug in a newspaper column, over 900
readers wrote to her. When Janice Guthrie's business
was mentioned in ''Reader's Digest,'' she received
over 740 calls immediately. The list goes on.

The media desperately want news. About 80 percent of
what you read in the papers is planted by people like you
and me sending out news releases!

How do you write a news release that works? John
Martin, a publicist with the ANDMORE Companies, writes
in ''How to Press Release,'' ''Have some news. It
doesn't matter what your news is. If you're opening a
new store, that's news. If you've hired a new sales
manager, that's news. If you've closed a big deal,
that's news.'' (For a free copy of Martin's booklet
containing sixteen rules for getting press coverage,
call 713-558-9900 or FAX 713-558-1880.)

Sending out your release is easy. First, think of
what your prospects read. That's where you want to send
your release. When Ron McCann of McCannics air
conditioning repair hired me to write a news release for
him, I of course sent it to the AC trade magazines. But
another way to send a release is through a wire service.
John Martin says you can send a 400-word news release
over his wire to over 2,000 media contacts—for only
$600.

> 1995 can be your year of rip-roaring prosperity if you start to help yourself by helping the media. Feed them news and watch them feed you free publicity!
>
> BIO: Joe ''Mister Fire!'' Vitale is a marketing samurai known for getting results. He is the author of several books, including ''The Seven Lost Secrets of Success,'' ''Turbocharge Your Writing,'' and, for the American Marketing Association, ''The AMA Complete Guide to Small Business Advertising.'' Contact him at mrfire@blkbox.com or call 713-999-1110 or fax 713-999-1313.

for his booklet within days after the article appeared. In fact, he had to go and reprint more copies of his little gem. A few of the people hired him to write press releases for them. Many of them actually asked him for my phone number. Talk about a win-win for all! "Free" remains one of the most powerful and persuasive words in our language. Maybe in any language.

4. *Notice that the column offers solid information.* This not only tells people why they should write news releases, but it tells them how. There's enough information here for any reader to try writing a release, but it doesn't give away the farm. (We'll discuss how to write online e-releases in another chapter.) Prospects who want to achieve success with the media will no doubt call the experts: the people mentioned in the column. A rule of thumb in writing this type of "sales letter" is to give 95 percent information and 5 percent plug. Give readers enough exciting information so that they feel they are tasting the steak you are cooking for them. And then pull the plate from under them, making them ask you for the rest of the meal.

5. *Notice that the column ended and began with a bio and address info about the author, me.* This made it easy for any readers curious about my services or books to contact me—which they did. I had prospects e-mail me about my writing services from Australia, England, Mexico, and Canada.

6. *Also notice the format of the text.* There aren't any capitals shouting for attention, or any unusual margins, or too many

changes in text structure. This makes it easier for online readers to move through the e-text.

7. *Finally, notice that the column doesn't feel or look like a sales letter*. That's the key. Online potential buyers like to buy but don't like to be sold. If your sales piece looks like a sales piece, many readers will skip your message, delete it, or flame you for it. That's why it's so important that you write a "disguised" sales letter. Don't list any ordering information. Let prospects ask you how to order from you. This approach is similar to writing newspaper ads in an "editorial" style. Because readers are skeptical of ads, placing ad copy in a format that resembles a newspaper story tends to increase readership. By disguising your sales letter, you are accomplishing the same thing online.

How to Write a Special Report

Writing books, booklets, articles, and special reports as a promotional device isn't new. Businesses have been doing it over a hundred years. Knowing that people like information, coming out with an "info product" is a proven way to build credibility for your service while also promoting it. This technique has never been more powerful than it is online.

Think of what your customers and clients want to do and why they come to you. Then pick some aspect of that subject and turn it into a special report. For example, if you're a tax attorney, you might write a report titled, "Ten Ways to Beat the IRS This Year." ("Ten ways" to do anything is a sure-fire easy way of writing virtually any report.) If you're a florist, you might write a report called, "The Right Flowers to Send for Every Occasion." The idea is to create a short, benefit-rich article that people will want to read; and while they are reading it, they are thinking that you are the expert because you wrote it and because the examples in it just happen to plug your services. Your report, in essence, will become your sales letter.

One of my clients has a college funding service. He looked at all the ads on CompuServe and complained, "There are dozens of people posting 'Cash for College' ads on there!" He added that they were all selling a computerized scholarship service, and not offering a truly beneficial service to college-bound people. I advised him to create a special report titled, "The Truth About Those 'Cash for College' Ads!" By creating such a report, he'd separate his service from all those other ones online. And because people online devour information, they would eagerly download his report and then, later, call him for his services.

Here are some examples of booklets and reports from real businesses:

- Guarantee Mutual Life came out with "How to Protect Your Business."
- Savings & Loan League came out with "How to Stretch Your Dollar."
- National Football League came out with "Official Record Book."
- American Cancer Society came out with "You Can Fight Cancer and Win."

You can create a special report that offers real information to people while also plugging your business. Something as short as 400 words (about two typed, double-spaced pages of text) would suffice. Think of how your service benefits people, and then write an article that helps them perform that service for themselves. If you're a plumber, it might be "Five Ways to Keep Your Drains From Clogging Up." This is acceptable advertising online. When people read your report, they learn definite, helpful information. They don't learn enough to replace you, however. So when they have a plumbing problem, you are the person they think of to call!

Yet Another Disguise

Your sales letter can also take the form of a press release. When Steve Armstrong of The Virtual Book Shop asked me to help him promote his online bookstore, I suggested he use a press release rather than a traditional sales letter. Knowing that his potential online prospects wanted information, I felt that an information-rich press release would serve as a disguised sales letter. We'll discuss press releases in depth in a later chapter, but I want to introduce them to you now because of their potential use as a marketing piece. Figure 3–5 shows the press release I

Figure 3-5

News from Awareness Press Service
Contact: Joe Vitale
Phone: 713-999-1110
For Immediate Release
Sell more books online? This bookseller does!
   (Rocklin, CA. November 1, 1995)—While most
booksellers are either wondering whether the Internet
will help their sales or complaining that it doesn't
help at all, Steve Armstrong is laughing all the way to
the bank.
   Armstrong sees 250 to 300 customers browsing the
online catalog for his Virtual Book Shop every day. And
he's getting five to seven orders a day, seven days a
week, with an average order of over $100.
   What's his secret?
   ''Everyone wants his or her own shop online, and
that makes it tough on customers,'' explains
Armstrong. ''It's far easier for people to visit just
one big bookstore and search for what they want there
rather than trying to visit a hundred little stores.''
   The Virtual Book Shop currently lists more than
40,000 books from over thirty booksellers, two
publishers, and four magazines from Australia, New
Zealand, Canada, England, the Netherlands, Italy and
the United States.
   ''When customers want a particular title, books by
a certain author, or a list of books in a subject, all
they have to do is stop at my online store and type in key
words for what they are looking for,'' says Armstrong.
''A complete search happens in seconds, and for free.''
   Armstrong wants his World Wide Web (WWW) site to be
the most complete selection of out-of-print and hard-
to-find books and magazines online. Though he's been in
business online only since November of 1994, already
his location has become a hot spot among booksellers and
book buyers. America Online is creating a direct link

to the Virtual Book Shop, and Worldata, Inc., is setting up a link to the ''Encyclopedia Britannica.''

''I'm making this store the definitive place to shop for hard-to-find books,'' says Armstrong. ''I'm currently writing a software program to allow buyers to send their credit card information in an encrypted, secure format. When that happens, look out. Sales will explode. People will be buying books like crazy.''

Many booksellers with WWW sites are complaining that they aren't selling books. Armstrong says the problem is having too many shops for potential customers to visit.

''I'm living proof that if you put every related product under one roof online, people will come,'' says Armstrong, who invites booksellers to contact him about listing their catalogs in the Virtual Book Shop.

You can reach Steve Armstrong at 1-916-632-9770 or by sending him e-mail at admin@bookshop.com. Or write 2351 Sunset Blvd., Suite 170-307, Rocklin, CA 95765. Visit the Virtual Book Shop at http://www.virtual.bookshop.com.

wrote for Armstrong. Note that it doesn't sound or feel like the type of sales letter you might find in your mailbox at home or even at work. Instead it has a credible newspaper "feel" to it, and that's what online prospects welcome.

"Spamming"

In the real world you can rent a mailing list of prospects from a mailing list broker and mail your sales letter to everyone on it. Try that online and you'll probably earn an e-mailbox jammed with flames. You'll also risk earning an online reputation you'll never erase in this lifetime. Word travels fast in cyberspace.

But that fact won't stop a lot of people. Two now infamous lawyers claimed they made several thousand dollars by "spamming" a sales post and sales letter to every e-address they could wrench off cyberspace. They neglected to mention the number of flames and even death threats they received. Or that they were kicked off of at least one online service provider. Their reputation is still in critical condition.

The term "spamming" comes from a Monty Python routine where every meal at a restaurant comes with Spam, no matter what was ordered. Spamming means posting a sales letter or any e-message to any and all e-lists, or mailing it to any and all e-addresses, regardless of whether your message is relevant or not. It's a major violation of the etiquette of online commerce. Don't do it. Ever.

You'll gain far higher results by targeting your prospects. Find the people who would be most interested in your services. Post messages where they lurk. Advertising cigarettes to non-smokers would be ridiculous offline; it's just as ridiculous to post your sales letters in areas where no one cares. Pinpoint your market. Your product or service isn't for everybody, so take careful aim and locate the Usenet groups and e-mailing lists where your prospects are gathered. Go fishing where the fish you want are biting.

Some companies are starting to provide e-mail addresses to businesses, just as offline mailing list brokers do. Promote-a-Page's Direct E-Mail, for example, can e-mail a message about your website or service to thousands of Internet users who have voiced an interest in your specific subject matter. This provides an instantaneous and effective way to get a lot of quality traffic to your business. The cost is about ten cents a name. (See **http:// pub.savvy.com/promote/** for details.)

There even now exists a software program called Floodgate that will read postings in Usenet groups and strip out the e-addresses for the persons who wrote the posts. It then creates a database of e-addresses to which you can send your sales letter. If you have a service of interest to entrepreneurs, you might let Floodgate read the posts in the Usenet group *alt.entrepreneur* and copy all the e-addresses from everyone who recently posted something there. You then have a database of entrepreneurs toward whom you can aim your sales letter.

A better way to collect a file of e-addresses is to have a form on your website that allows people to sign up for your mailing list. Just add a statement that says "Click here to join our free mailing list." When people add their names and e-mail addresses to your file, they are saying that they want to receive information from you. You can then flamelessly send them press releases, sales letters, and other relevant materials.

But be careful. Most people online do not like to receive unsolicited mail. The only way to soften your letter's unannounced appearance in their mailbox is by adding a personal note, something like: "If this is coming to you in error, please delete it. I understand that you are an entrepreneur looking for new opportunities. This may interest you."

At least then you have paved the way for your letter. If the person reading your note is truly an entrepreneur looking for new opportunities, he or she will probably read on. Again, if you haven't focused on your prospects, you could still send something unwanted and find yourself in flame hell. Always target your messages.

Summary

Cybertravellers still feel resistance to nuclear sales attacks. When they see a traditional sales letter online, they feel as if the text is screaming at them, and the response isn't pleasant. The Information Highway wants exciting, new, involving information in the style of the column I posted. People on this highway don't mind products and services being softly plugged within the context of the piece, but they typically rebel against obvious sales copy. Unless browsers have asked for your sales literature or visited your website to learn more about you, do not hit them with heavy sales artillery. Instead, offer practical information given in an easy and entertaining style.

One way to look at this is to think of advertising your business in the newspaper as opposed to sending a news release about your business to the newspaper. The paper will run your ad if you pay it. But send your ad to editors and they'll trash it. They don't accept "ads" as news.

Same with cybernauts. They don't want your ad, but they welcome your information. In short: The best way to write an effective e-letter is to give online readers stimulating information related to your service in a format they welcome and can read.

4

How Would Mark Twain Handle E-Writing?

How would Mark Twain write online?

Although it's anyone's guess, I like to think Sam Clemens would apply his techniques as a speaker to the world of cyberspace. Most people don't realize that Mark Twain became famous for his speaking talents. His skills as a journalist and a humorist made him popular, but it was his speaking that shot him into fame. Later, his books made him a household name. But even then, Twain's speaking engagements kept him in the public eye and helped secure his place in American history.

But Twain wasn't a born speaker. If anything, he was born to navigate boats. As an author and as a speaker, Twain was self-taught. He worked hard to perfect his skills as an orator. He learned by watching such greats as Charles Dickens and by paying attention to how charismatic ministers held the attention of their congregations. Twain also learned from his own mistakes.

After reading all of Twain's published speeches and looking for the common elements in them, I think he used six secrets in making himself famous. And I think you and I can use these same methods when we're writing in cyberspace. I believe just playing with these six techniques will improve our cyberwriting and make our online experience all the more enjoyable.

Secret One: Rehearse

Mark Twain once quipped that it took him three weeks to make a good impromptu speech. Although Twain's speeches gave the appearance of being done spontaneously, they were actually well thought out, even written out, rehearsed, and committed to memory. His goal was to achieve what he called "counterfeit impromptu."

In other words, he was so prepared that he appeared unprepared. It was planned spontaneity. This gave him a lot of power. He knew what he was going to say down to the exact pause, and this allowed him room for improvisation while giving him the security of knowing what he was going to say next.

Twain was like an actor. He wrote out his speech, or script, committed it to memory, and rehearsed it. When he strolled on stage, he moved with an ease that made him appear to be totally relaxed. While the audience thought he was talking to them informally and spontaneously, he was actually delivering a well-planned theatrical performance. In fact, it was so perfectly theatrical that virtually no one ever guessed that Twain had planned the event days or weeks in advance.

In short, Twain's first technique was one of preparation. Many speakers today think you should never write out your speech because it makes your talk rigid, but it's important to realize that Twain didn't read his speech or even repeat it the way he memorized it. He used his planning as a base for his performance. He gave himself permission to ad-lib, to stray from his talk, and sometimes to leave it altogether. But this initial preparation made him more comfortable and helped him give a more powerful, humorous, and satisfying talk.

How do you apply this to cyberwriting?

One of the biggest mistakes cybertravellers make is to write their material quickly and zip it off without rewriting it, editing it, or even rereading it. Anything you write for the online world needs to be as polished as anything you write for publication. It's very easy to dash off a response to someone and send it off. The problem is, the potential for miscommunication is enormous. And when you consider the fact that your e-message can potentially be read by millions of people, there's cause for alarm. You don't want a written blunder to get broadcast around the world.

To protect yourself, keep these suggestions in mind:

1. *Know what you want to say.* Don't waste everyone's time trying to guess what you mean. Ask yourself, "What do I want to say? What's the one message here?"

2. *Pretend you are speaking to one person who is sitting across the desk from you.* Mentally role-play a dialogue that begins, "Here's what I want to say . . ." Write your monologue down.

3. *Now edit.* Whittle your message down to the essential points. Pretend you are writing a telegram and every word will have a price tag on it. The more words you cut out, the less the message will cost you.

The first secret, then, is to rewrite and perfect your e-writing before you ever post or send any message.

Secret Two: Cheat

The second trick Twain invented for himself was a "cheat sheet."

When he first began giving talks, Mark Twain was terrified that he would forget his speech. He began by walking out with his entire written speech in hand and placing it on the podium. But he quickly learned that he could never see the manuscript while he moved around. He needed something more concise.

His next step was to write out key words to remind him of each of his stories. He would lay this sheet on the podium. He quickly learned that all the words looked alike from a few feet away, and he couldn't keep his place on the page. He kept forgetting where he left off. He needed something more effective.

Finally, Twain stumbled across the idea of using pictures. He would draw a little doodle that represented the story he wanted to tell. He placed all these doodles on a page and left the page on the podium. One glance and he could recall in an instant what he wanted to say.

Surprisingly, this is the same method being taught in schools today by leading teachers and proponents of left-right brain theory. Twain somehow intuitively knew that he was tapping into a very visual part of his brain when he made his drawings, and this page of drawings was all he needed to switch on the logical part of him—the part that would remember and tell the stories.

So Twain's second trick was developing an easy way of remembering his talk, a way that didn't require a lot of preparation or a pile of manuscript pages on the podium.

How do you apply these methods to cyberwriting?

Before you write anything for online use, think through what you want to say. Make an outline, or a series of doodles, to help you frame your message or your argument. Writing and posting messages without regard for what you want to say or how you want to say it is one of the biggest reasons people get flamed. If you take the time to consider your message before you write a word of it, you'll lessen your chances of miscommunication.

I often use a scratch pad and write out key words before I actually start to write any e-message. The "cheat sheet" helps me focus on my message and stick to the point. It also assists me in remembering everything I want to say. How many times have you thought of a great line after your conversation is over and your partner has left the room? Writing down key words to help me remember my key points makes my actual writing smoother. It also helps me relax, as Mark Twain's notes helped him relax, because no matter what happens during the course of your communication, you have your cheat sheet to fall back on. It will remind you of what you want to say next.

Secret Three: Use Creative Expression

Twain's third technique involved showmanship.

He knew that style was more important than substance, at least in giving a talk. Many authors read from their famous works, but Twain learned that their approach seemed wooden and dead. He once saw a minister hypnotize a congregation by using dramatic and emotional devices. Twain never forgot it.

One of Twain's tricks was to use pauses. Every good speaker knows that a pause can be very powerful. While Twain told a story, he would pause just before delivering a punch line, or just before giving the surprise ending. This pause made his conclusion so dramatic that it was often electrifying.

Another trick was to speak slowly. Twain spoke with a deep drawl, one so slow that a reporter said Twain spoke at the rate of three words a minute. That's an exaggeration, but it gives you an idea of Twain's well-paced delivery. Again, he was rehearsed. He could have spoken faster if he had wanted to. He had learned that pauses and pacing made for a more engaging performance.

Twain's third technique, then, was creating a style that was all his own, one that engaged the audience and kept their attention.

How do you apply this to cyberspace?

Because the online world is ruled by ASCII text, you might think that your style will be hampered. Not necessarily true. Ernest Hemingway, Jack London, Ray Bradbury, Connie Schmidt, and many other legendary authors had only typewriters and one font to express their personality, yet their writing style is recognizable even today. The message here is to write in your own unique voice, not to worry about being considered literary or sophisticated or even "businesslike." You want your own voice to shine in your cyberwriting.

You accomplish this by allowing your creativity free expression. When replying to a message online, why not allow yourself the freedom to express your answers in more creative ways? I once corresponded with a woman who answered her messages as poetry. Her style was her own. Another person always began and ended a message with a relevant quote from someone famous. These little tricks made their otherwise dull ASCII text come alive, and made their style colorful and memorable. Twain would have loved it.

Let yourself be yourself. Forget pleasing English professors or sounding important. Say what you have to say in your own way, always focusing on clear communication, of course, but also letting your own personality shine. Since so many people online write with a stiff or ambiguous style, your personal and clear writing will leap off the screen and be remembered. You can also employ visual tricks to help readers "pause" when they read your words: Ellipses, dashes, and short sentences all help convey a sense of ease in your online communications.

Secret Four: Weave Stories

Twain's fourth technique was actually one of the "lost secrets" I wrote about in my book on marketing, *The Seven Lost Secrets of Success.*

Twain was a storyteller. He was a storyteller in print as well as on stage. He knew that nothing held people's attention better than a well-told tale. Many of Twain's 700-some talks were nothing more than stories and short tales. Some of them were about his adventures overseas. Some of them were rewritten stories from his books. But they were virtually all stories.

It's worth mentioning that one of the few complaints ever aimed at Twain was that his stories held little or no meaning. Critics complained that he was a humorist without a message. That's debatable. But it's worth thinking about. Stories move people—and a story with a purpose can change people. When it comes to selling online, you want your stories to have meaning. When they do, they'll persuade.

A lack of message may have been Twain's only shortcoming as a speaker. But again, his goal was to entertain, not to enlighten. And as an entertainer, he was enormously successful. His talks and tales are remembered and discussed even today, a hundred years after he wrote many of them. His place in history—his story—is secure.

You can apply this method to your e-messages by remembering to tell a brief story or two when answering a question or posting a message. For example, when I was hired to write an online ad for a book, I didn't simply say, "New book." Instead, I told a brief story about a man who read the book and was so grateful for it that he called the author and thanked him. Stories bring life to your communications.

The only caveat here is remembering that the online world wants your messages to remain brief. People will read anything as long as it interests them. But go one line into boredom and they'll stop reading. Any story you tell has to be interesting to work in cyberspace.

Your stories also have to be relevant. Telling a funny story in your sales copy won't help you sell anything unless the story somehow drives home a point that relates to what you want to sell. Telling a story in any e-message that doesn't add to what you are trying to communicate will be seen as needless clutter.

Secret Five: Use a Starter

Mark Twain's fifth technique was what he called a "starter."

Twain loved to fully engage his audience as soon as he

stepped on stage. He wanted to start the program on the right foot by capturing the audience's attention and keeping it nailed on him. He developed several clever ways to accomplish this:

1. His favorite starter was the self-introduction. Twain would simply walk on and introduce himself. This usually made the audience warm to him right away, and it saved Twain the trouble, he said, of training people to introduce him right.

2. Another popular starter was walking on stage and saying nothing for a full minute. Sixty seconds of silence is a *long* time when you're on stage and an audience is waiting to hear you speak. This trick made people laugh, chuckle, wonder, and guess what Twain was up to. But it certainly held their attention.

3. The last starter Twain used was walking on stage with a book and acting as if he were going to read from it. He would open it, but then close it and begin to "ad-lib." His "ad-libbing" was actually his well-planned talk. Because people expected Twain to stop at any moment and return to the book, they paid attention. They felt that he must be saying something more important because he was delaying reading. But Twain never returned to the book. He simply used it as a device to make people focus on him.

In later years Twain didn't need a starter at all. His reputation as a speaker was so well known that all he had to do was step on stage and people were smiling and hanging onto his every move and word.

How do you make this method work in cyberspace?

Let me answer with an example: Say you are about to reply to a message concerning a new delivery system that someone asked you about. You begin your message by saying, "Here's what you wanted to know about our delivery system . . ." But then you stop and redirect the message with a new statement: " . . . But before I tell you about it, let me mention something about our new overnight service."

What you've done is capture people's attention, and then hold on to it. They'll wait and read on because they expect you to return to your original statement and complete it (and of course you should return and complete what you start). This is a powerful way to use Twain's technique and keep people riveted to the screen.

Another method I've used is called "the plunge." You begin your e-message right after something has happened and before people fully grasp what you are talking about. Good fiction uses this technique. The story begins with gun smoke floating up from a revolver, someone dead, and someone else running out the door. "What's happening?" ask the readers, and before they know it, they're reading the entire story. The opening "started" them.

You can apply the same method to online communications by starting your message where other writers might have their third paragraph. In other words, most online writers take too long to get to their point. Most of them could delete the top half of their message and lose nothing. I suggest that a good starter would be to begin your message where others might have their third paragraph. If you get a message beginning with the words, "He looked shocked when we told him the sales reports," you'd probably read on to find out who was shocked, why he was shocked, and what the sales reports actually said.

Consider starting your message in places where readers are forced to read on to discover what is going on.

Secret Six: Participate

Twain's sixth and last speaking technique will be the hardest to describe as well as emulate online.

Twain had "presence." You've seen photos of him. His loose hair, piercing eyes, typical white dress, cigar, nose, and bushy mustache made him stand out from the crowd. But Twain also had a presence about him that made people look at him. It's said he once went to a party and when he walked through the door the host asked, "Who in the world is *that?*"

Twain's presence was felt on stage as well. Part of anyone's presence is due to his or her reputation. When Twain was a best-selling author and famous speaker, audiences paid him a great deal of respect. His presence was in their own perception. But Twain's manner and dress also gave presence, and that's something any speaker can learn from. Twain dressed differently, walked differently, and spoke differently. All of this gave him presence.

How do you apply this in the e-world?

Cyberspace seems to strip people of rank and status. When you're online, you're seen as just text. The surest way I know of for creating your presence in cyberspace is by being in cyberspace a lot. In other words, be active. Participate. When you're on e-mailing lists, reply to messages. Post ads to newsgroups. Take an active part in online activities and discussions. As people see you, they will come to know who you are. Your online presence will create an online presence. In short, your online writings and contributions will create an online presence for you.

You can also add to this presence in creative ways. Sam Clemens became "Mark Twain" partly to add color to his personality. I use the moniker "Mister Fire!" for the same reason. People remember the name "Mister Fire!" It helps make my online presence more notable and memorable. Think of ways to make your online appearances more noteworthy.

Summary

Apply Twain's speaking techniques to your cyberwriting and you'll see dramatic and immediate results. As Twain himself noted, "A successful book is not made of what is in it, but what is left out of it." The very same could be said for your cyberwriting. Polish to perfection, edit ruthlessly, and *then* send your e-message to the world.

5

The 1903 Secret for Making Millions Online

I first read about this secret in *The Psychology of Advertising*, a 1903 book on advertising written by a famous business psychologist of the day.

Dr. Walter Dill Scott said that everyone collects something. He said it was a built-in natural tendency. He said we *have* to do it. What we collect is up to us. Dr. Scott said there's an unconscious reason that we collect things. Most of the time it has to do with wanting to feel secure, or safe, or smart, or different. For the purposes of this book, it doesn't matter at all why anybody collects what he or she collects. All that matters for you and me is that this is a basic law of human nature.

Three Teaching Tales That Prove the Point

You'll better understand this secret—and the awesome power of it—once I tell you three stories that illustrate how this principle works.

Story One: SRV

I am a fan of Stevie Ray Vaughan, the Texas blues-rocker guitar player who died in a helicopter crash in 1990. My love of SRV runs deep. His powerhouse music has saved my soul and raised my spirits. Because of how I feel about him, I started collecting his music. His commercial releases are easy to get. You just walk into a music store and buy them. There are also two videos for sale and two biographies of him. I have it all, of course (and even helped the author of one of the biographies write her book). But a true collector doesn't stop there.

I let people know that I am an SRV fan, and they let me know who has rare recordings I might buy or trade for. Over time I have acquired quite a bit of SRV music, from rare audiotapes of him giving early concerts in small clubs, to videotapes of him in Japan or Canada. Recently I even discovered a company that has an entire library of bootleg video- and audiotapes of SRV, all of which they sell for a modest price. For die-hard SRV fans like myself, it's the cookie store of my dreams.

Story Two: Old Advertising Books

I am addicted to reading old books. Subjects I am most interested in are advertising and marketing, and especially any books on the psychology of persuasion. Since I am collecting these types of books, I stop in every new bookstore I see, I ransack out-of-print bookstores, and I even hire professional book locators to hunt down specific books for me.

I'll pay any price, too. Once a person faxed me a note saying she had a copy of a 1925 book on advertising. She wanted fifty dollars for it. I immediately wrote a check. Another day a company in New York City said it had found a copy of a book printed in England on copywriting. I of course sent the company a check.

When will this stop? True collectors never stop. As long as people keep producing new materials on advertising, or finding old ones, I'll never stop.

Story Three: The Pencil Lady

I know a woman who collects pencils. That's right, pencils. I have no idea why she wants a collection of pencils, but that's her chosen obsession. When I had a booth at a convention in Houston a couple of years ago, she desperately wanted me to get her a commemorative pencil. When I was jogging at a local park and found an unusual pencil on the jogging trail, I gave it to her. She was thrilled!

There's no end in sight for her madness, either. As long as there exist pencils she hasn't seen yet, she'll hunger for more. And as long as people keep making pencils, she'll keep buying them.

How to Profit From People's Instincts

People collect things. So what? What this means is that you and I can profit from this principle to a staggering degree. Let me simplify the principle and then explain it:

1. Find out what people collect.
2. Offer them more of it.

Step One: How to Discover What People Collect

It's easier than you think to find out what people collect. First you can check the Usenet groups and online mailing lists. People known to be interested in something join a list of similar-minded people. For example, people interested in marketing probably subscribe to one of the e-mailing lists for discussions of marketing.

Or look at my obsession with SRV. In the real world, there is a SRV Fan Club. (Yes, I'm a member.) If you want to let SRV fans know of something you have concerning SRV, you can rent that subscriber list. Online there isn't yet an SRV fan club, but there exists an active e-mailing list devoted to the discussion of SRV's music (to join, send the message "subscribe" to *texasflood-request@dmu.ac.uk*), another dedicated to blues music, and several Usenet groups that pertain to music.

So step one in this process is to pinpoint collectors. In other words, find a large group of people who are collecting something in particular. If you already have something to sell, locate the groups that have an interest in your product or service. If you want to create a product or service, get involved in a few online groups and follow the discussions. See what people are interested in, what their concerns are, and so on.

Step Two: How to Make Money by Supplying More of What People Collect

Now offer them more of what they want. This is easy, too. If you can find more of what they want, great. But chances are this may be more work than you think. SRV is dead, for example, so finding more of his material might be tough. But you can create more material.

If you want to make millions off SRV fans, create something about SRV for them to buy. There's already a biography of SRV out. But that didn't stop Keri Leigh, an Austin blues singer who knew Stevie. She wrote a book on him, too. And of course it's selling. It's selling because SRV collectors want it.

So the real key here is to create more of what people already want. If they are collecting books on advertising, write a new book on advertising. If they are collecting pencils, create a new pencil.

This is actually the basic concept behind any good business. Find out what people want and give them more of it. But Dr. Scott's insight is clearer than anything I've ever come across before. People collect. Find out what they collect. Offer them more of it. If more isn't available, create it.

The Real Secret Is Information

What are the most popular products for most online collectors?
Information products.

Information products are books, tapes, videos, and even software. But you don't have to go to that extent. All you really need is a special report. And the beauty of this strategy is that a special report is easier to write than a book, takes less time than a book, and can net you more money than a book!

It took me two years and several thousand dollars to write *The Seven Lost Secrets of Success*. I sell it for $12.95 a copy. It takes me one day to write some of my special reports. I get $10 for every one I sell.

But there are more benefits for you when you write a special report. First, you are considered the expert on the subject you wrote about. People still bow to authors. I'm regarded as an expert on success because I wrote a book about it. I'm regarded as an expert on advertising because I wrote a book about that, too.

But I'm also regarded as the expert on writing because I wrote a twenty-two page "book" on the subject, and the expert on service because I wrote a twelve-page special report on it, and the expert on writing sales letters because I wrote a nineteen-page special report on that, too.

And all of this credibility brings me more business. Hermann Hospital in the Houston Medical Center hired me to write a fund-raising letter. The American Red Cross hired me to create a marketing plan. Two major companies out of state hired me to write articles and sales letters for them—all because I'm considered the expert. And I'm considered the expert because I wrote some information products to satisfy people's need to collect.

How to Find Your Customers

First: Target a group of people already collecting something. Look online for collectors. And when I say look for collectors, I really mean look at what specific groups of people are interested in. A person who buys a weight-loss product by mail won't call himself a "collector" of weight-loss products. But offer him another weight-loss product and he will probably buy it. People don't think of themselves as collectors, but they are.

How to Create a Hot Product

Second: Create an information product for that group. You can't give the group fluff, of course. Any special report would be worthless if it weren't based on a proven formula for accomplishing something. This can be easy, too. Just write up a short but usable report on how this group of people can do something they already want to do.

For example, people buy books on golf. Write a special report on how to play the game better. Think of something no one else has and write it up. Those golfers will collect your new book, too.

One way to learn what has been done before is to visit your library and browse *Bowker's Subject Guide to Books in Print*. (Or see **http://www.amazon.com**.) If you intend to create a new item for golfers, for example, look under "golf" and scan all the titles. See what has been done before. Then see what you can come up with that hasn't been touched yet. Create a new special report for golfers with valuable information in it and they *will* buy it. Why? Because they collect material on golf!

How to Make Them Buy Your Product

Third: Offer your product to the group of collectors by means of a small e-ad. If you advertise, be sure you write a killer ad and place it where your target audience is going to see it. If you ad is weak or placed in the wrong area, it will flop. If it doesn't grab and persuade, few will respond.

Your e-ad can also take the form of a post in an appropriate e-mailing list. You can nonchalantly mention that you have a new report on how to (fill in the blank) and people can contact you for more information. The only way to be sure you won't get flamed is to be sure your post is relevant to the group reading it. If you've done your homework, you should be placing your posts in the right areas.

An Example: Going Fishing

One of my clients runs a video and television production company in San Antonio, Texas, called Alan Warren Outdoors. The owner of the business said he wanted to go online but didn't know where to begin. I urged him to step back and first consider his reasons for wanting to go online. Developing a presence in cyberspace is one thing, but developing a profitable one is another. He needed a strategy. We discussed the possibilities and the potential problems. We decided that the best purpose for going online would be to increase awareness of his television

programs and his sponsors' products and services. The only
question now was how. Here's how I approached it.

Step One

I checked the following sources to locate his target market
online:

1. A quick browse through *The Internet Resource Quick Reference* turned up such Usenet groups as *alt.fishing* and
   rec.outdoors.fishing and *rec.hunting*.
2. And then a quick search at **http://www.tile.net/listserv/**
   led to the e-mailing list FLYFISH, devoted to flyfishing.
   (To subscribe, send e-mail to *listserv@ukcc.uky.edu* with
   the message "sub FLYFISH *your name*.")
3. And a search at **http://www.neosoft.com/internet/paml/**,
   a directory of publicly accessible e-mailing lists, led to
   two other groups devoted to fishing and the great outdoors.

Step Two

I **lurked**, or quietly observed the posts, on those areas for a
couple of weeks, read the FAQs pertaining to those groups, and
got a feel for the nature of the discussions. I noticed that blatant
ads were not permitted. I also noted that people would openly
express their enthusiasm for a camping area and others would
usually flame them to death. These people could be ruthless.
Some complained that the posts were about too many saltwater
spots, while others complained that the posts were about too
many freshwater fishing holes. You couldn't win. It was clear
that commercial messages would not be accepted in these
groups. Still, I continued to lurk in order to get a better understanding of how my client could develop his online presence.
Here's what I finally suggested:

1. *Develop a website devoted to hunting and fishing that would
be updated on a regular basis.* Since the primary subjects of interest
of his target audience appeared to be "where to hunt and fish"

and "techniques for hunting and fishing," I suggested that he focus on providing this type of information. And in order to encourage repeat visits to his website, I suggested that he update this information weekly, if not daily. I also urged him to make his site interactive, allowing viewers to vote on their favorite places to fish, and inviting them to add new places not yet mentioned at the site. If viewers could add their own comments, they would find the site more interactive than other sites. If they could read what others had to say about fishing and hunting, they might find the site more interesting. Again, I wanted a site that was interactive, interesting, and fun.

2. *Forget posting any ads to the Usenet groups.* Given the nature of the groups, I felt this was way too risky. Instead, I urged my client to let his television audience know of his website. This would be a powerful way to turn his existing viewers into regular online visitors. If they liked it, they would tell others. All my client had to do was add a tag to his commercials giving the URL to the website and inviting viewers to visit it.

3. *Continue monitoring the Usenet groups to learn more about what his potential customers were interested in.* This was simply good reconnaissance work. The resulting information could be priceless. By paying attention to what people were looking for, he could quickly add what they wanted to see to his website. If people suddenly seemed interested in fishing holes in Alaska, he could just as quickly add that information to his website.

4. *Talk to his television sponsors about putting links to his website.* In other words, my client's sponsors could create their own websites, advertise them, and create hyperlinks to other sponsors as well as to the main website belonging to my client. This would create a synergistic event. Whenever people visited any of the websites, they would at least see a link to my client's website. This is networking online at its best.

I also suggested that my client create a special report titled "The World's Most Effective Fishing Lures." This report could be posted at his website, listed with all the search engines, and made available to anyone looking for that kind of information. The more helpful and interesting his website, the more "hits," or visitors, his site would see.

The last time I checked, my client was working with an Internet provider to develop the website I proposed.

Map to Success

While this might seem like a long way to go to make a sale, it's really the most direct route to success for closing sales online. This map leads to gold.

To give you a parallel example, another client of mine said he loved a businessman's free fax-on-demand service. He said, "I spent an hour calling his fax and requesting all his free documents. Then I read them. And then I found myself wanting to order and collect all the products he mentioned in his reports."

This is how the 1903 secret works online, too. You find people already collecting what you have, and you let them know you have more. Because of their inborn need to collect, they almost can't help themselves from contacting you . . . and then from ordering from you.

Example: Pathfinder's Success

Tom Mulkern runs an online business supplying information to cybertravellers. The first thing he does to make money online is locate the people who are known to want his type of product. He looks for people collecting money-making how-to books and reports. Most of them can be found in the business forums and classified ad areas of online services across the planet. Mulkern places a simple ad online to fish for the people most likely to be his prospects. Here are the headlines he uses, in order of best results:

1. HOW TO MAKE MONEY ONLINE!
2. FREE ONLINE MARKETING REPORT!
3. START OR GROW YOUR BUSINESS ONLINE!

Figure 5–1 shows the ad he runs on CompuServe, America Online, and Delphi, and in about twenty Usenet groups. It works as a lead-generating ad. Short and to the point, it delivers

Figure 5-1

> Online marketing is a hot topic these days . . . and
> for good reason: the benefits are remarkable! You can use
> online marketing to grow the profits of your existing
> business, start a home-based ''cyber-business,'' or
> gain the edge on your competition through research and
> communication.
>
> But in order for you to take full advantage of this
> amazing technology, you need to understand exactly
> what works and what doesn't . . . from a *marketing*
> perspective. We've spent the better part of three years
> researching online marketing and successfully selling
> a variety of products and services.
>
> Save yourself the agony of the ''experimental
> learning curve'' we went through and get our FREE Online
> Marketing Report. Just send an e-mail message to:
> report@mulkern.com
> Your report will be delivered within seconds by our
> auto-responder. Thanks for reading this post.
> Yours for Online Profits!
> Tom Mulkern, President
> Pathfinder Publishing Group
> http://www.mulkean.com/pathfinder
> Tel (508) 388-8813
> Fax (508) 388-8337

enough information for people to decide whether they want to
know more. Anyone who collects how-to reports about marketing online will no doubt act on the offer and zip off an e-mail
note to Mulkern's **mailbot** (an automated e-mail reply service).

Within seconds the person who replied to the ad will receive by e-mail the sales letter shown in Figure 5–2. Note that
this letter comes close to being a very traditional sales letter. The
big difference here is that people are asking for this letter, and
Mulkern reminds them of that fact right off the bat.

Mulkern's letter works. He has sold over 400 copies of his
manual online within six months and says his letter brings a 5

(*text continues on page 93*)

Figure 5-2

Hello!
    Here's the free report you requested! This has been
sent to you by an ''auto-responder,'' but if you have
any questions, just e-mail pathfinder@mulkern.com or
call our office at (508) 388-8813. We're here to help
with your online marketing!
    Tom Mulkern
    Pathfinder Publishing

    ''How You Can Very Quickly Master Online
   Marketing and Use It to Successfully Start or
       Grow Your Business Online''
Dear Friend,
    I'd like to thank you for requesting this report. As
you already know, online marketing is a hot topic these
days. Why? Because the barrier to entry is nonexistent
and the profit potential is unlimited!
    Right now, you can start profiting enormously by
tapping into this rapidly expanding electronic
marketplace that already numbers 30 million strong and
is expected to *explode* over the next several
years. . . .
    You can use online marketing to earn extra income
from home, develop an additional profit center for your
business, network with other entrepreneurs and
associates, save time and money in sending documents,
or simply for research and communication.
    You can deliver your sales messages online to highly
targeted groups for rock-bottom cost. You can get
started by placing simple classified ads or lead-
generating messages for a few dollars . . . and FREE in
many cases!
    If you have an information-based product, you can
even arrange to have it delivered to your customers
online with no involvement from you. Of course, the same
can be done for answering inquiries from prospects and
questions from customers.

You can test product ideas, ads, headlines, offers, and copy and get answers almost instantly . . . compare this with the WEEKS of waiting to test a traditional marketing campaign. . . .

And of course, you can run an online business from anywhere—your home, an executive office park, or on a tropical island! You are not confined by place or time—all that matters is the RESULT you produce. Through your computer and modem you are connected to a global marketplace that is growing at an astonishing rate.

Still . . .

Even with all of these benefits, many people are finding they are not making as much money as quickly as they'd like. The reality is, your online marketing efforts may turn out to be a huge money maker . . . OR A DISASTER!

If you've done any research at all into this, you're probably being bombarded with information from all kinds of folks claiming you can make a fast fortune on the Information Highway.

Unfortunately, many people have fallen for the hype and overexaggerated claims of promoters who have never even sold anything online!

Make no mistake, there are a lot of people out there who are charging outrageous sums of money for electronic marketing information and ''gimmicks'' that are absolutely useless!

That doesn't mean that electronic marketing is not an enormous breakthrough. It is. But just like any business, there is a ''recipe for success'' in electronic marketing.

If you don't have all the right ingredients, and put them together in the right way, you'll have the same success rate you'd have if you tried to bake a cake without a recipe. Zero.

But if you know the ''recipe for success''—and USE it—you're going to discover that it is possible to make

(continues)

Figure 5-2 (continued)

thousands of dollars a month online for very little work!

WHERE CAN YOU GET THIS RECIPE
FOR ONLINE MARKETING SUCCESS?

Well, you can spend thousands of dollars and several months of your life trying to cut through the hype and the technical mumbo-jumbo to figure it all out.

Or you could waste your money on a get-rich-quick scheme or those overpriced reports and courses by the so-called experts that contain a ton of fluff and very little usable information.

OR, YOU COULD DO IT THE EASY WAY!

By learning the ''inside secrets'' from someone who has actually been profitably selling products and services electronically for almost two years. Someone . . . like me!

As an entrepreneur and marketing consultant, I'm always looking for ways to increase advertising exposure and lower costs, so I naturally became fascinated when I heard about electronic marketing.

I got started almost two years ago when I made a $600 profit from my very first $13/week ad on Prodigy. From then on I've been hooked!

And after spending several months and thousands of dollars on electronic marketing books and courses, and going to live seminars, I realized there was a crying need for some straightforward, specific and USABLE information that would help the average person or small business owner start making money with this tremendous opportunity.

You see, online marketing is not about plundering a virgin market with ill-conceived sales messages . . . that will only serve to alienate the very market you are trying to serve! It's not about ''getting rich'' off the Information Superhighway or ''making a killing'' on BBSs [bulletin board systems] (although you very well might).

It IS about dramatically changing the way you conduct business. It's about automatic-pilot, systematized prospecting. It's about the affordable and efficient ATTRACTION of people who can benefit from your products and services (and are ready, willing, and able to buy them NOW).

Effective online marketing utilizes many different techniques including multi-step lead generation, and selling through educating your prospects and providing valuable information.

You can quickly use these methods to REVOLUTIONIZE the ways you get new business and keep your customers coming back for more.

Because it reduces advertising and prospecting costs, and speeds up sales, it literally allows you to get more results from less effort.

And because of the AUTOMATED features of online marketing, it drastically reduces the amount of time you need to spend from the initial point of attracting a prospect until the time it takes to make a sale.

''How can you learn the techniques that
REALLY work right NOW?''

Well, I'm pleased to tell you that I've spent months boiling down everything that works in online marketing into a step-by-step marketing system. The result is an exciting guidebook called, ''The Online Marketing Action Plan: A Step-by-Step Guide for Creating an Electronic Profit Machine!''

Unlike newsletters and reports that give you information piecemeal and have you going in fits and starts, this book gives you an 8-point ''master plan'' for success on all of the online services, BBSs, and the Internet! Here are just some of the things you will learn in this powerful book . . .

* Why it is crucial to define and pinpoint your online market first, before you start selling (this is where most electronic marketers go wrong right at the start).

* Learn the demographics of the people on each of the online groups (Internet, Commercial Services, and BBSs) and how to use this information to find the best

(continues)

Figure 5-2 (continued)

products to offer them. Before you try to sell to this
market, first you have to understand it!
* Learn the right way to market on the Internet and how
to get the Internet crowd to accept you as welcome guest
(instead of an annoying pest!).
* How to write e-mail letters *effectively* so you can
convert the leads you'll be getting into orders! (This
is where most online marketers are failing miserably
and it's the MOST IMPORTANT element of online
advertising.)
* How you can start with twenty dollars' worth of ads
and be getting orders online within forty-eight hours!
* The hottest way of selling right now on the World Wide
Web and how you can get in on it for less than you'd ever
guess!
* The proper way to use an auto-responder (or mailbot)
and how to direct so many inquiries to it; your ''mail
robot'' will be working harder than a legion of postal
employees . . . without costing you a dime!
* A six-step method for creating your own best-selling
info-product using online research. All the
information you need to create powerful information
products is a few keystrokes away . . . if you know how to
find it!
    There's more: You'll learn how to get the rights to
hundreds of high-quality info-products to sell online
if you don't have one already. . . . How to get your ads
posted on GEnie, AOL, Prodigy, and Delphi—without
having to join all those services! . . . How ''lurking''
can be a very profitable use of your time. . . . How to
slash your CompuServe charges by up to 80 percent while
REDUCING the amount of time it takes to respond to
leads. . . . How to make your classified headlines and
other postings jump out and force readers to contact you
before they contact anyone else. . . .
    And even more: you'll learn how to get FREE
publicity by placing special files in key places online
that will multiply themselves and create a ''snowball
effect'' of orders. . . . How to send electronic press

releases for FREE that could potentially result in millions of dollars worth of business. . . . The best ''point and click'' software for marketing on the Internet and how to get it for FREE. . . . Why most small ''BBSs'' are a waste of time and which ones to focus on for maximum results. . . . How to take an online winner to the traditional media and make possibly ten times more money . . . and much, much more!

Listen, there's a ton of other dynamite information packed into this book that I just don't have the space to cover here. It's all specific, to-the-point information you can use right NOW to promote your product or service or create and sell your own info-products.

This type of ''desktop'' direct marketing via online technology is the wave of the future. Take a look at what one of the top advertising experts for the American Marketing Association has to say about my book:

''Tom, your book is awesome—clear; well-written; packed with tips, tricks, and insights that anyone can use. I haven't seen anything this clear-headed and street-smart in ages, and I've NEVER seen anything this complete for online business. You ought to call this 'The ULTIMATE Marketing Guide'—it is!''
—Joe Vitale, author, ''The AMA Complete Guide to Small Business Advertising'' and ''The Seven Lost Secrets of Success''

And here's just a brief sampling of the dozens of other *unsolicited* comments I've received:

''Mr. Mulkern, your manual was great! It helped me to get up and running in one day. This straightforward course in nontechno language was a godsend. In fact,

(continues)

Figure 5-2 (continued)

using your techniques, I was in profit within two
weeks!''
                          —David Legletieter, Manhattan, Kansas

''I have purchased other online marketing materials,
and yours was by far the most impressive—I've paid
more for a lot less. Thank you for a truly superior
product at a fair price!''
                          —Stephen Speaks, CompuServe member

''I couldn't wait to tell you what I thought of your
work—it is an EXCELLENT piece! By far the most
complete, informative, and interesting to read among
the online marketing material I have purchased both
online and off. This is the ONLY manual anybody who is
interested in online marketing has to have! It's a
pity I didn't run across your ad earlier—you could
have saved me hundreds of dollars!
                          —Alberto Bueron, Ontario, Canada

    This big 157-page, 8½ × 11 manual comes in a spiral
binder so you can use it ACTIVELY. It is written in
nontechnical language and gives you a proven, step-by-
step system for implementing winning electronic
marketing projects, and then AUTOMATING the whole
process . . . so you can enjoy all the money you've made!
    This material is ''cutting edge'' intensive and you
just won't find anything as usable on the market for any
price. But with our manual, you can get it all in one
place, and . . .
           YOU CAN GET IT ENTIRELY RISK-FREE!
    ''The Online Marketing Action Plan'' has sold
offline for $69.97. However, since you are already a
fellow ''cyberpreneur,'' we'll give you $30 off IF you
order immediately!
           That means it's yours for only $39.97!
    Keep in mind that I've seen others charging hundreds
of dollars for much LESS information than you will find
in my manual. Everything that currently WORKS in

electronic marketing is boiled down into a simple
marketing system that anyone can follow and use right
NOW!

Everyone else is giving you ''picks and shovels.''
I'm offering you the ''golden nuggets!''

100 PERCENT UNCONDITIONAL GUARANTEE

I personally guarantee this book 100 percent. If
this material doesn't help you earn hundreds of times
its low cost, send it back for a full refund anytime! No
questions asked and no hard feelings either. I feel so
strongly that this book can help you I'll back it with a
LIFETIME guarantee, PLUS . . .

Three Additional FREE BONUSES!

Also, if you do order within the next seventy-two
hours, not only will you get the special low price, we
will also include the following bonuses:

* FREE Bonus #1: ''Writer's Dream'' shareware that you
can use immediately to create your own disk-based
informational product or order-generating report
(it's extremely easy!).

* FREE Bonus #2: ''How to Profit From the Coming World
Wide Web Marketing Explosion!'' This ten-page special
report (hot off the press) tells you exactly how to
profit from the Web and includes information on how you
can get your own Internet and World Wide Web ''Business
Presence'' at a FRACTION of the price others are paying!

* FREE Bonus #3: ''Electronic Marketing Resource
Directory.'' This is a comprehensive directory giving
you all the contact names and addresses of electronic
marketing experts and technical service providers that
can help you launch your CyberBusiness into orbit!

And these bonuses are yours to keep even if you later
decide to return the manual! Let's face it—that's a good
deal.

IT'S EASY TO ORDER

To order ''The Online Marketing Action Plan: A Step-
by-Step Guide for Creating an Electronic Profit
Machine,'' for just $39.97 plus $6 shipping and

(continues)

Figure 5-2 (continued)

handling, simply take out your credit card and call our
twenty-four-hour toll-free order line at:
                    (800) 536-7836
    If you prefer, order by e-mail by sending a message
containing your name, address, credit card number and
expiration date, and the words, ''send me #IN39, Online
Action Plan.'' Or fill out the form below and fax it to us
with your credit card information (or mail it with a
check).
    If you have any questions, please feel free to
e-mail me or call my office directly at (508) 689-7426.
Yours for Online Profits!
Tom Mulkern

P.S. As with all breakthroughs in business, the people
who get in on the ground floor will make the most money.
Right now, the window of opportunity is open for you to
join us in this cyberspace money-making revolution
that is taking off right under your nose. But that
window won't be open indefinitely. And remember: my
IRON-CLAD guarantee is actually BETTER-THAN-RISK-
FREE! You have nothing to lose, so order now!

© Copyright 1995 Pathfinder Publishing.
---------------------cut here ---------------------
                  NO-RISK ORDER FORM
        For fastest service, fax to (508) 975-3749
          Or Call 1-800-536-7836, Product #IN39
[ ] Yes! Please send me ''The Online Marketing Action
Plan: A Step-by-Step Guide for Creating an Electronic
Profit Machine.''
    I am ordering with the understanding that if I am not
absolutely astonished by the valuable information and
strategies it contains, I can return the manual at
anytime for a 100 percent unconditional refund.
Further, all of the FREE BONUSES are mine to keep no
matter what!
    On that better-than-risk-free basis, here is my
order:

```
[ ] I am ordering within seventy-two hours. Please
include all bonuses.
[ ] Enclosed is my check or money order for $45.97.
[ ] Please charge my credit card for $45.97.
cc# _____ exp. date _____
Cardholder signature
_____

Name _____
Address
_____
City              State             Zip _____
Country _____ Phone _____
Fax _____ E-Mail Address _____
Mail your order to: PATHFINDER PUBLISHING GROUP
          P.O. Box 505, Amesbury, MA 01913
          (508) 689-7426 Fax (508) 975-3749
          E-Mail: pathfinder@mulkern.com
* MA Residents please add 5 percent sales tax.
** Canadian orders please add $5. Overseas orders
please add $15.
          (U.S. Funds Only)
```

to 8 percent response. Not bad. What he has on his side is the fact that people online eagerly collect the information he offers. And as you know by now, collecting is almost an addiction for most of us.

Summary

Satisfying people's wants has always been a proven formula for business success. Dr. Scott's insight into human behavior can help us here. Find out what people are already collecting and give them more of it. Because the online world has so many Usenet groups, forums, and special interest e-mailing lists, locating people with specific interests is easy. You can even do searches to hunt down particular groups of people. All you have to do next is create something that caters to their already existing passion for more.

6

Net-Advertorials: How to Tell and Sell Your Story Online

In 1896, Charles Austin Bates, one of my mentors and one of advertising's founding fathers, wrote that good advertising ". . . is simply telling a plain story. It consists merely of giving information to possible buyers."

Not many in advertising would agree with that definition today, yet it is one of the soundest explanations of how to get attention (and sales) in cyberspace. If you can write about your product or service in a low-key, informative way, you will win friends and possibly make sales. One of the best ways to do just that is something called the "net-advertorial."

As you might guess from the name, an "advertorial" blends an advertisement with an editorial. The added "net" lets you know this is for the Internet, or any online service. If you can imagine writing a news story about your product or service, including details about how to do business with you, and posting this story online, you have a clear idea of what a net-advertorial looks like. It offers more news, less sell.

Net-advertorials are a way to flamelessly let the online world know about your product or service. You can post them in the appropriate Usenet groups, offer them to pertinent e-mailing lists, and send them to people with whom you exchange e-mail.

A PR Wizard's Technique

Murray Rogow is a seventy-year-old publicity genius who bills himself as "The world's SECOND greatest press agent."

(P. T. Barnum and Ziegfield tie for first place, he says.) Rogow has been writing press releases offline for nearly five decades and online for the past few years. I interviewed Rogow and asked him to reveal his procedure for writing press releases that get read. Knowing the basics can help you write net-advertorials that stand out in the crowd. Here are his pointers:

1. *Being a good publicist starts with being a good journalist.* Being a good journalist means knowing the five *W*'s and the *H* . . . Who, What, Where, When, Why, and How.

2. *Learn how to write the inverted paragraph.* Always assume that no matter how much you write, an editor may clip off your story from the bottom, and a reader may never get beyond the first paragraph. It is mandatory that you write all the truly essential information in the first forty to fifty words. That way, if someone reads only the first paragraph or two, you at least have communicated your essential message.

3. *Begin with a headline that is a digest of what the story is all about.* If the headline is filled with puff adjectives, it's going to turn people off.

4. *Always give a date for when you wrote the release, and a contact name and number.* This is important in case people want more information.

5. *Always give a source.* If an editor or reader needs to verify a fact or wants more information, he or she needs to know whom to call and how.

A Rogow Basic Lesson

Pretend you need to write a press release about a guest speaker talking on a fairly interesting subject. Write out answers to the five *W*'s and *H*. For example:

Who:	Mr. John Jones, noted business authority
What:	Will speak on how to invest in a business at ABC Business Club
When:	Day, date, time, A.M. or P.M.
Where:	Holiday Inn, location, city

How: [*There is none in this example*]
Why: [*There is none in this example*]

You can write a release for this example in two ways, says Rogow.

1. If the speaker is more important than the topic, mention him first.
2. If the topic is more important than the speaker, mention it first.

Here's how Rogow would write the release for the first approach:

> John Jones to Speak on ''How to Invest in a
> Business'' at [*Month/Date*] Meeting of ABC
> Business Club
>
> [*Your town, state*]: John Jones, noted business
> authority, will speak on ''How to Invest in a
> Business'' at the monthly meeting of the ABC
> Business Club to be held on [*date, time*] at [*name of
> hall, address*]. For more information call
> [*number*].

"If you think like an advertising person and write in advertising-ese," Rogow warns, "you will fail to get into print. If you follow the 5-*W*'s and the *H*, you will be a big success . . . online or off."

Elements of the Net-Advertorial

The net-advertorial is a relatively new form of writing for online readers. It is more than a press release and less than an advertisement. It combines a news angle with a soft-sell approach. Here are some suggestions on how to create your own:

1. *Make it look like a news story*. Remember the "editorial" part of the definition. This particular form of writing has to be in the style of a feature news story. Read the features in your newspaper to get the feel of good journalistic writing. Although your piece is intended to sell, the selling has to come across as news. Again, the online world values relevant news above all else. If readers smell "sell" in your story, you may get flamed.

2. *Deliver news*. Find what is new in your product or service, and focus on that. If a newspaper reporter were going to write a story on your business, what would he or she focus on? Find the news and center your story on it. Genuinely inform readers. Give more information than what you would in a typical offline news release.

3. *Give quotes*. Again, good newspaper stories strive for a well-rounded view of a story. They look at other sides. They get opinions. One way of having quotes from others included in your story is to add testimonials from satisfied people.

4. *Give contact information*. You don't want to focus on how people can call you to order your product, but you can include details on how you might be reached. A tip here is to include these details somewhere inside the story, and then repeat them at the very end of your story.

5. *Make paragraphs short*. News stories are typically broken up into one- and two-line paragraphs. Copy that form so that your piece has the look and feel of something found in the newspaper.

6. *Get to the point fast*. The focus of your news should be in the first few lines of your story. Journalists give the most important news first, then use later paragraphs to expand on the news. Your net-advertorial needs to follow the same formula. Don't make online readers have to work to discover your message.

7. *Refrain from using emoticons*. Not enough people online know that :) means happy face or [] means hug, so don't use these smileys in your text. You should also refrain from using such acronyms as ROFL (Rolling On Floor Laughing) or OTOH (On The Other Hand) because these may also cause confusion and not help your communication. Keep "netspeak" to your

personal online communications with people who you know understand it.

8. *Never double-space.* Double-spaced e-text takes up too much bandwidth (think of it as cyberspace transmission lines) and looks hard to read on the screen. However, on longer posts such as net-advertorials, adding a space between paragraphs makes reading easier and your post more visually inviting.

9. *Say something "negative."* Advertisements are notorious for claiming that the product or service advertised is the best. Yet we all know that the product or service must have some flaws. You can create credibility in your net-advertorial by admitting a flaw. Say something negative about your news item, and readers will tend to believe everything else you say. Focus exclusively on the positive, and you and your post will be regarded with suspicion. After all, a reporter writing about your business will almost always find something weak about it. Maintain this news-oriented stance and add something apparently negative about your product or service.

Net-Advertorial Samples

Figure 6–1 is a sample of a net-advertorial. You can easily see that something like this could be posted in the Usenet groups or e-mailing lists concerning health or weight loss, cooking, or possibly even in the groups dealing with books.

The net-advertorial shown in Figure 6–2 has been successful as an ad on e-mail lists, where permitted, and as a press release where ads are not permitted. In the latter case, the author just deleted the paragraphs with prices and phone numbers. It has appeared as "special interest group" postings on American On-line and as "forum" postings on CompuServe. It never fails to sell books. For the record, the author also gets an occasional workshop attendee enrolling in response to it (at $700 a pop).

How I Write E-Releases That Win

When someone hands me a product to promote, I look for the story into which it fits. Let's use a book as an example. I don't

Figure 6-1

Austin Texas (March 17, 1995)—Need to watch your fat intake but don't have the time to compute all the fat in your next meal?

Have no fear. A new book by a woman from Austin, Texas, may save the day.

''The Low-Fat Times—Delicious Recipes 20 Percent Fat and Less'' ($13.95 from Karen Associates, Inc., 13492 Research Blvd., Suite 120—224; Austin, TX 78750) takes the bother out of choosing and deciding what low-fat food to cook for yourself or your family. The 278-page soft-cover book comes divided into nine easy-to-follow sections, from chicken and turkey recipes to soups and vegetables.

''All the recipes in the book are 20 percent or less in fat content,'' explains Karen Cole, a full-time legal secretary who wanted a cookbook with less fat content than the 30 percent or less the American Heart Association suggests.

''It was a hassle to work the fat formula for every meal,'' Cole said. ''In my book the fat formula has already been worked out for you so you can go ahead and forget your calculator!''

One of the most important and unusual features of the book is the way the recipes are described. Cole has divided each recipe into groups. This way, she says, you don't have to worry about what order to do things. When the recipe says ''Add Group One,'' you simply look at the list for that group and put them together.

At the end of each recipe Cole lists the nutritional information for that meal. Included is the total amount of fat, calories, protein, cholesterol, carbohydrates, and even sodium.

''This is not a diet book,'' Cole said, ''though you could use it as one. Instead, this is for people who are conscious of fat and want to keep their fat intake within a healthy percentage.''

Although Cole would rather go motorcycling or

Figure 6-1 (continued)

> bowling than cook in the kitchen, she said she feels
> that a lot of people like herself will want the
> information in her book.
>   ''We're just too busy to stop and figure out formulas
> or worry about fat,'' she said. ''But it's something we
> have to do to remain healthy. I hope my book helps others
> achieve and maintain a healthy lifestyle.''
>   The only thing missing in her book is a good index.
> Apparently the author trimmed it out of her book when
> editing for the fat.
> ''The Low-Fat Times—Delicious Recipes 20 Percent Fat
> and Less'' ($13.95 from Karen Associates, Inc., 13492
> Research Blvd., Suite 120–224; Austin, TX 78750)

want to write a press release to promote "a book" as that usually isn't much news, but I probe to learn how the book fits into a larger picture.

For example, let's talk about the fellow who got a call from a reporter eight minutes after he faxed out my release. His book is called *Fun Projects with Wooden Pallets.* If I were like most publishers, I might whip up a release saying the book was now out and say a little about it. But I don't think that's very powerful. I prefer a double-whammy approach, which I achieve by combining the new book release with a feature story approach. After some thought I came up with the following headline:

New Ways to Make Furniture—and More—From Scrap

Note how that headline has a more "news feel" to it? It doesn't even mention the book. That, to me, isn't as important as what the book helps you do. In advertising we talk about features and benefits. The book is a feature; what you can do as a result of having the book is the benefit. I focused on the benefit.

The next thing I looked for was a killer opening line. I believe that the first line in your feature news release should be a grabber. If you don't hook the editors there, they probably won't go on to the rest of your release. It's worth mentioning right here

(text continues on page 104)

Figure 6-2

''This is the most astonishing and generally
convincing book on sales that we've read.''
                              —''Success'' Magazine, May 1995
FAQ: What's the Difference Between High-Probability
Selling and Traditional Selling Methods?

High-probability selling is the first new sales
paradigm in the history of selling. It's based on
extensive research into the sales performance
characteristics of highly successful salespeople.
It's what they actually do, their attitudes, beliefs,
and behaviors. It's not what they THINK they do.
    We've worked with hundreds of salespeople, and only
a rare few can accurately tell you what they do on sales
calls or what the probability is that a specific customer
will or won't buy. We identified the common threads of
their successful behaviors. We've organized, codified,
tested, and constantly improved on the model.
    The most startling of our research findings is that
most highly successful salespeople (earning well over
$100K) don't use ANY of the sales tactics that we have
all been taught to do and seem logical enough.
    They don't prospect by ''selling the
appointment'';
    they don't make sales calls with the intention of
making a sale;
    they don't do ''rapport'';
    they don't flatter or try to charm anyone;
    they don't make multiple calls to ''build
relationships'';
    they don't ''find needs and solve problems'';
    they don't educate their prospects;
    they never ''assume the sale'';
    they don't persuade or convince prospects to do
anything they don't already want to do;
    they don't tolerate uncooperative or evasive
prospects;

(continues)

Figure 6-2 (continued)

they don't compromise their dignity or self-respect;

they don't do great presentations;

they don't try to ''earn the prospect's business'';

they don't ''overcome objections'';

they don't use ''closing techniques'';

they never ''ask for the order.''

So what DO most highly successful salespeople do?

They make appointments ONLY with prospects who want to buy and are willing to buy from them. That requires a different attitude and different communication skills than most salespeople understand. It's not a selling process; it's an identification and disqualification process. The way they present their offering creates trust and respect instead of suspicion and resistance.

In ALL of the following steps they will DISQUALIFY the prospect as soon as the prospect does anything to indicate that there isn't a very high probability (statistically: about a 90 percent confidence factor) that he or she will do business. They do it courteously, and they may arrange to come back at another time, but they never knowingly waste time with a low-probability prospect.

They determine whether they trust and respect the prospect early in the first visit, and whether it is mutual. They go on sales calls with the intention of quickly determining whether there is a mutually acceptable basis for doing business; if not they disqualify the prospect. They know how to form deep emotional bonds quickly. If that doesn't happen, they disqualify the prospect and go on to the next prospect.

They find out exactly what the prospect's buying motives, buying intentions, and product/service requirements are. They find out who participates in the decision-making process and require the prospect to arrange for him or her to talk to all concerned.

They find out who must approve the purchase and require the prospect to arrange for him or her to talk to all concerned. They learn exactly what is the normal procedure for the prospect to make a purchase, whether it's how they get a purchase order issued, or who writes the checks, or who signs the contract.

If they are confident that they can meet the prospect's requirements, they immediately seek a conditional agreement to do business. That's the first commitment.

Once conditional commitment is made, they negotiate their mutual conditions of satisfaction. In other words: they negotiate the specifics of their product or service, what it can and can't do, what's acceptable and what's not. They write down what the prospect is agreeing to buy, and both get a copy. That's the second commitment.

If they need to, they prepare a proposal. They come back with the proposal and review the conditions of satisfaction and reconfirm the prospect's commitment to buy before the prospect sees the proposal. That's the third commitment.

They show the proposal, or do a presentation or demonstration of their product with the prospect, to confirm that they actually meet the specific conditions of satisfaction. That's the fourth commitment.

They complete the transaction. That's the fifth commitment.

Are there highly successful salespeople who use traditional selling methods? Yes, of course. But, why would you want to? This book is a pleasant and interesting reading experience.

''High-Probability Selling Reinvents the Selling Process''
by Jacques Werth and Nicholas Ruben, 1995, 198 pages, $19.95. To order with a thirty-day unconditional money-back guarantee of the purchase price (not the shipping cost of $4.00), call our toll-free number with a Visa or MasterCard.

1-800-394-7762

For more information about the book, sales training

(continues)

Figure 6-2 (continued)

> workshops, or sales and sales management consulting,
> call 1-800-394-7762.
>   To talk to Jacques Werth, call 215-657-0770.
>   e-mail: HiProbSell@aol.com
> ''High-Probability Selling Reinvents the Selling
> Process''
> ''This is the most dramatic development in selling that
> I've seen in my thirty years in the business.''
>   —Phil D'Achille, V.P. Sales
>   and Education, Prudential
>   Insurance and Financial
>   Services

that your editors will decide to read your release—or not—
based on your headline. If it intrigues them, they'll read on. But
the next potential stopping point for them is your first line. In
the case of the above client, my first line was this:

> You know those wooden pallets stacked up in and
> behind many businesses?

That's an opening line that I still love. Why? It gets readers
nodding their heads, saying "yes" internally, and puts them in
a receptive mood. It also pulls readers into the next paragraph.
It makes them ask, "What about those pallets anyway?"

From there I created a story about how to use the pallets to
create furniture—the news—and I quoted from the book and the
authors, thereby plugging the book within the context of the
feature story. Do you see the difference? Rather than focusing
on the book, I focused on the story and mentioned the book
within the story.

The client for whom I wrote this net-advertorial said he had
a reporter call him only eight minutes after he released my story!
And that reporter turned the story into a five-column feature
article on the front page of the Sunday newspaper, complete
with photographs as well as the name, address, and phone number for ordering the product. Figure 6–3 shows the entire story
as I wrote it.

The short release for Harley-Davidson shown in Figure 6–4

Figure 6-3

New Ways to Make Furniture—and More—from Scrap
   (Silsbee, Texas. September 1, 1995)—You know those
wooden pallets stacked up in and behind many
businesses?
   According to ''Fun Projects Using Wooden Pallets''
($14.95 postage paid from Applecart Press, P.O. Box
612, Silsbee, TX 77656), a 115-page, fully illustrated
new book by Don and Peggy Crissey of Silsbee, Texas, you
can pick up those pallets, usually for no charge, and
turn them Into over a hundred easy, practical, and fun
home projects, such as beds, chairs, fences, planters,
toys, steps, and tables, to name just a few of their
uses.
   ''There are over 460 million pallets made each year
in this country,'' says Don Crissey, an engineer with
over twenty years of experience in recycling
everything from government surplus paints to ocean
cargo containers. Crissey adds that 53 percent of these
pallets are used once and then discarded.
   ''What people don't realize is that half of the
expensive hardwood cut down goes into making these
pallets,'' explains Crissey. ''That means there's some
very fine and expensive wood in those pallets—wood you
can use to make some beautiful furniture.''
   According to Don and his wife Peggy, a former retail
shoe store display designer, a single pallet can fit in
the trunk of most cars, and each pallet can be easily
turned into any of over a hundred simple, fun, and
practical do-it-yourself home projects.
   ''We spent three years picking up pallets and using
the wood,'' said Don Crissey. ''I've made everything we
describe in the book, from benches to beds to utility
cabinets. Our front lawn has planters, steps, and
chairs sitting on it, and no one ever realizes they were
all made from pallets!''
   ''Besides the joy of making these projects,'' adds

(continues)

Figure 6-3 (continued)

Peggy Crissey, ''it feels good to know you are doing
your part to be earth-friendly.''
      For a free sample of directions on how to make one
project from a wooden pallet, send a self-addressed,
stamped envelope to Don and Peggy Crissey, Applecart
Press, P.O. Box 612, Silsbee, TX 77656.
      To order the new book ''Fun Projects Using Wooden
Pallets,'' by Don and Peggy Crissey, send a check or
money- order for $14.95 (postage paid) to Applecart
Press, P.O. Box 612, Silsbee, TX 77656.

was so powerful that CNN read it and profiled the company only three days after its release.

A Review of Tips on Writing Net-Advertorials

These points are so important that I think we should review them again:

1. *Create a riveting headline.* Editors will often decide whether your piece is interesting or not on the basis of the headline alone. Make sure it is a grabber. You want a one-line statement that pulls them right into wanting to know more.

2. *Write a catchy one-line first paragraph.* I once began a release saying, "Janice Hedlund wonders why lawyers go home at night and juries get locked up." It compelled the editor to keep reading. The line I wrote for the pallets book (above) teased readers into wanting to know more. This first line is another make-it-or-break-it point for editors. Make it hypnotic.

3. *Spell out the essence of the story in the next paragraph.* Journalists, online or not, are accustomed to getting all the facts right away. Give them the essentials—who, what, when, where, why, how—right here, in the second paragraph. This helps them decide whether your story is one they want or not. And keep in

Figure 6-4

FOR IMMEDIATE RELEASE
Contact: Mr. Ed Dombrowski, Harley-Davidson of
Stamford, Inc.,
    hd.stam@ix.netcom.com, 203/975-1985
    Dr. Clifford R. Kurtzman, The Tenagra Corporation,
    Cliff.Kurtzman@Tenagra.com, 713/480 6300
HARLEY-DAVIDSON ENTERS THE FAST LANE ON THE
INFORMATION HIGHWAY
    Stamford, CT, April 27, 1995—Internet users can now
put on their helmet and leathers, fire up their engines,
and get out on the information highway with Harley-
Davidson of Stamford, Connecticut. Harley-Davidson of
Stamford, Connecticut, today announced the official
opening of its World Wide Web information center and
storefront that allows Internet riders to experience
the Harley lifestyle and culture.
    Located on the World Wide Web at url http://www.hd-
stamford.com/, the Harley-Davidson of Stamford
website provides a forum for Harley-Davidson
enthusiasts to view the Harley-Davidson and Buell
motorcycle lines, visit the parts counter, learn
service tips, purchase clothing and collectibles,
browse a calendar of upcoming Harley-Davidson events,
and enter the Racer's Corner. Visitors can also submit
pictures of themselves on their Harley to win a Harley-
Davidson T-shirt, and listen to the sounds of Harley
cycles and download Harley video clips.
    ''We wanted to convey the excitement of being part
of the Harley family to those out on the Information
Highway,'' said Ed Dombrowski, Sales Manager for
Harley-Davidson of Stamford. ''We developed our web
presence to create a dialogue between our company and
Harley enthusiasts worldwide. We believe that Internet
users, like Harley owners, are on the cutting edge, and
that this medium provides an outstanding opportunity
for us to interact with our loyal audience.''
    The Harley-Davidson of Stamford website was

(continues)

Figure 6-4 (continued)

> created in partnership with The Tenagra Corporation
> http://arganet.tenagra.com/, a company in Houston,
> Texas, that specializes in Internet marketing
> strategies. According to Dr. Cliff Kurtzman, President
> and Chief Executive Officer of Tenagra, ''The challenge
> of this application was to create an entertaining
> website that conveys the look, feel, and sounds of
> Harley-Davidson to its Internet visitors. We relied on
> providing substantive content along with an exciting
> graphical interface to achieve that objective.
> Internet visitors won't be able to smell the rubber
> burn, but they should be able to imagine that they
> can!'' C'mon and Ride!

mind that journalists usually will not print your story as you deliver it to them. What your release does is "pitch" an idea to them that, if you did your job right, will interest them enough to write and print their own version of the story. Putting the essential information up front helps a reporter decide what is important and respects time restraints.

4. *Use quotes.* It's worth repeating that quotes bring life to your stories. A rule of thumb is to have a short quote every other paragraph. Rather than writing out a narrative, change the narrative into a quote by a key person in the story.

5. *Make the story brief.* Tell a full story, focusing on one idea or message, and do it in fewer than 400 words. If you write anything longer, you're creating a feature article and not a net-advertorial. Be brief. Respect reporters' time. If they want more information in order to write a longer story, let them contact you.

6. *Give contact information.* Be sure your name, address, phone, fax, and e-mail addresses are all on the release. Also, add this contact information at the top of your release *and* at the bottom, so that no one has to scroll through online text to find it.

7. *Personalize your release.* Online releases should be less formal. If you are e-mailing your net-advertorial to someone you know, add the line, "John, thought you'd like this one." This is equivalent to scribbling a handwritten note on a paper release. It brings attention to what you are offering. If you intend to post your net-advertorial to a Usenet group or e-mailing list, be sure to soften its introduction with a few opening words. Something such as, "I've been busy these days working with clients. I thought everyone here would enjoy this press release, as it brings you up-to-date on what we've been doing." Your personalization makes your net-advertorial much more acceptable online.

8. *Snail-mail a copy.* It's easy to lose online stories. Help editors by also sending them a snail-mail copy of whatever you are e-mailing them.

9. *Use simple words.* One of my associates keeps writing releases that sound as if a college professor wrote them to impress his peers. The average reading level for the American public is the sixth grade. Don't use multisyllable words if shorter, better-known synonyms exist; don't use uncommon or unfamiliar words. If you don't hear the words used in everyday conversation, don't use them in your online releases. Although reporters may understand sophisticated words, their readers may not. Be simple.

10. *Write many one-line paragraphs.* Make your writing easy to follow and visually attractive. Look at how newspaper reporters write stories. Many of their articles consist of nothing but one-line paragraphs. These are elementary for people to follow and understand. They also make for rapid reading. Apply the same ideas for the same reasons to your e-releases and net-advertorials.

WWW *Sites for PR Help*

"Press Release Tips for PR People" by Andrew Kantor, Senior Editor, *Internet World* magazine, is at **http://www.tenagra.com/releases. html**.

"A Quest for Insight: PR in Cyberspace" is a twenty-two-page insight-

ful report on what journalists look for. Read it at **http://www.
successful.com/report.html**.

"A Reporter's Internet Survival Guide" by Patrick Casey contains a
wealth of links to publications, resources, and more for filling your
press releases with solid information. See it at **http://www.qns.com/
~casey/**.

Where to Send Your E-News

For a priceless list of newspapers, magazines, TV stations, and
other media outlets that accept press releases by e-mail, see the
back of this book. You can always find the most current copy of
Adam Gaffin's list at **http://www.webcom.com/leavitt/medialist.
html**.

Summary

Think like a reporter and find the news angles in your business,
and then deliver that news to the groups or groups that would
have the most interest in it. The more you can focus on delivering relevant and timely information to people, the more those
same people will pay attention to you—and then pay you for
your services.

7

How to Write a CyberAd

For more than one hundred years, good advertising professionals have been using the same formula for creating their ads.
Known as "AIDA," it represents "Attention, Interest, Desire, Action": a proven structure for a successful ad. But the online
world requires a new formula. Use the old one and you're likely
to create an ad that will get you many replies: all flames. Why?
Online travellers prefer less direct forms of advertising. Although this prejudice is changing by the moment, it will be a
while before direct selling is accepted online. Until then, you
need a safer formula. I have one, and I call it "TARGET." Before
I tell you how it works, let me explain the three online ad formats that I think will work best for you.

Three CyberAd Formats

These little known but powerful formats can help you create
online ads that grab attention:

Format One: Imaginative

Bruce Barton, cofounder of BBDO, one of the largest ad agencies
in the world, often used a method for creating ads called "Imaginative." With it he wrote some of the greatest ads in American
history. In my book on Barton, titled *The Seven Lost Secrets of
Success*, I said that this method "reveals the business nobody
knows." It is a powerful way to write an online ad. Let me give
you a couple of examples.

In the 1920s there was an ad for a door that had the headline, "The Personality of the Doorway." The copy revealed why

a door was special, as well as what it revealed about the home and the home's owner. This ad helped sell more doors because it imaginatively revealed something typically unseen about doors. It went deeper than the obvious. Instead of merely saying, "Buy our doors," the ad made the product new and different. The ad was imaginative.

Back in 1925, when Barton was speaking before the American Petroleum Institute, he told the members of his audience that they were not selling gasoline at all. He said, "My friends, it is the juice of the fountain of eternal youth that you are selling. It is health. It is comfort. It is success. And you have sold it as a bad-smelling liquid at so many cents a gallon. You have never lifted it out of the category of a hated expense."

Look for what your product or service delivers. When people buy a drill, they don't want a drill, they want the holes the drill will help them create. But go deeper. Why do they want the holes? It may be to hang sentimental pictures of their family. It may be to help create a new room in their warm home. Use your imagination and focus on something deeper.

Format Two: Interpretive

This approach asks you to say something new about an old product. Create a fresh viewpoint. Someone selling soap might explain (as one ad did) "Your skin has five miles of pores. How clean are yours?" People reading that ad stop and say to themselves, "I didn't know that!" Your new information makes your product more interesting.

Recently, I saw a television commercial for a long-distance service that explained how a telephone call worked. It was interesting information that made me sit up and take notice where I might otherwise have paid no attention at all.

Think about your product or service, and consider the history of it and facts about it. What you take for granted may be exciting news to your readers. I once worked with a large motor repair company. I said the company should announce that it could fix any motor within one hour. My client countered with, "Any good mechanic can say that." I said, "But are the others saying it? If not, you have an opportunity to capitalize on a fact your peers take for granted and your customers don't know."

What is obvious to you that might be news to your prospects?

Format Three: Initiative

Confront readers with a direct question, and you're likely to involve them in your ad right away. That's why when you go to a movie theater the salespeople ask, "Large or small soda?" They assume you want a drink. They are taking the initiative in the sales process. When a salesperson asks, "Which do you prefer—a small car or a large one?" he or she is taking the initiative with you.

You can plunge a reader into an interaction with your product with this approach. For example, the most successful ad in history began with the question, "Do you make these mistakes in English?" The question yanked people right into the entire ad because it's involving, personal, and bold. It takes the initiative.

Think of your business and how you might write an ad that suggests and even demands involvement. Asking a personal, relevant, fascinating question can grab readers as they are whizzing by in cyberspace and pull them right to your ad.

Location, Location, Location

You can pick any of the above formats for writing an online ad. The TARGET formula will work for any of them. Just remember that online ads must be posted where ads are permitted, usually in business forums, appropriate Usenet groups, designated classified ad areas, or your own website. Post any ad where it is not welcome and you will get flamed. Again, read the posts in the area where you want to place your ad to get a feel for the nature of the information exchange there, and locate the FAQ for the area so you know what the area permits.

Just as in the real world, location can make the difference between failure and success in business. Put your retail store on a road with little traffic and you'll have a tough time selling your goods. The same concept holds true in cyberspace. Place your cyberad in the right location—in the appropriate area—or risk missing business and possibly gaining flames. The best ad will fail if posted in the wrong location.

The TARGET Formula

Now let's look at the formula itself.

"T" Means *Target* Your Prospects

The "T" stands for *target* your prospects. Far too many people online post their ads where they are not wanted. If you are offering a financial service, don't post it in one of the sex groups. If you are running a coffee shop, don't tell everyone on the mailing list devoted to computer programming. These people won't care. They aren't your prospects.

Target your ads by finding out where your potential clients are and posting your ads where those people will see them. Almost all advertisers think their product or service is for everyone, so they eagerly post messages online wherever they want. This clutters up cyberspace, wastes time, makes finding what people really want less likely, and frustrates and angers nearly everyone else. No wonder there's so some much flaming going on.

Pinpoint your market. Locate the gathering holes for your prospects and post your messages there. Have a multilevel product? Go to the Usenet groups allowing postings concerning that subject. Looking for a loan for your business? Go to the business groups that support your search. Have a product that appeals to joggers? Hang out in the discussion areas where you'll find joggers discussing their sport.

Here's a tip worth repeating: Although the majority of people online don't care for ads, they devour information. All you are being asked to do in this new formula is locate the people who should want your product or service, and not necessarily the designated safe areas to post your messages. In other words, find the spots where people are gathering to discuss something related to your product or service, and don't worry whether they allow ads or not. They all want information, and that's what you'll deliver.

"A" Means Get *Appropriate Attention*

A common mistake in nearly all advertising is tricking the reader into reading your ad with a clever, cute, or curious headline. Forget it. This doesn't work anywhere, but it creates even more damage online.

Imagine browsing through a series of headlines in a Usenet group. There may be hundreds in one group that seem, from their headlines, to interest you. But as you click on each headline and read the message, you find either (a) no message at all, because the writer forgot to post anything or made a mistake, (b) a short, ambiguous message that leaves you confused, because the writer neglected to give you enough details to know what he or she is offering, (c) an excellent post —very rare!—or (d) a message entirely unrelated to what you thought the headline suggested. Go through this frustrating process enough times in one evening and you'll wonder why anyone stays in cyberspace longer than a day.

You gain *appropriate attention* (the "A" in TARGET) by posting a headline that honestly refers to what you or your service offers. If you are an interior decorator, you might post a very direct message that says, "I make your business rooms look magnificent." The way to think of this is to imagine that you are a doctor and your service cures a problem. What's the problem you cure? Answer and turn it into a headline. If you are a person who creates business plans, you might write a headline that says, "Need money for your new or expanding business?" That headline refers to the problem that your service will solve.

Another way to create a headline people will read is to make it more informative or news-oriented. Using the business-plan fellow as an example, you might write a headline that says, "Three Ways to Raise Money." Because that headline sounds more like news and less like an ad, the chances of it being read are very high.

Focus on a problem that the reader has and hint at a solution. Your business cures something. What? When people come to me for marketing advice, they are saying "My business hurts." A possible headline for my own service might be, "Is your business slow?" If you have poor sales, you are my prospect, and you would see my headline, nod your head, and click your mouse to read the rest of my ad.

What does your own business do for people? Focus on their problem and generate a headline that readers will connect with.

Your intention here is to create a relevant headline, something that captures the appropriate attention of the people who would most be interested in your message. As advertising legends from John Caples to David Ogilvy have proved, out in the real world a change in headline can lead to nineteen to fifty times better replies. But a good headline online can capture up to (and over) 200 times more readers. Why? There are potentially more people online. What makes them decide to read your post/ad or not is—you guessed it—your headline.

Here are a few sample subject lines/headlines. Which would you want to read more about—and which would you delete without ever bothering to read the message?

HELP	or	Need Help With Windows 95
Need Money	or	Business Partner Needed New Company
Visit My Mall	or	New CyberMall Specializes in Antiques
Articles Here	or	Find Articles You Need with Search Tool
Sales Letters	or	How to Write a Million-Dollar Letter

"R" Means *Rouse* Their Emotions

The "R" in this TARGET formula refers to the fact that people buy for emotional reasons, not logical ones. They use logic to rationalize their decisions. Fill your ad with *rousing emotion* and you will move prospects in the direction of buying from you. Let me explain:

1. A blind beggar on the street corner wore a sign around his neck saying, "I am blind." He didn't get many people tossing coins into his cup until an advertising man changed the sign to read, "It is spring and I am blind."
2. A hot dog salesperson at a baseball game couldn't get people to move out of his path when he yelled, "Hot food coming through!" But everyone made way for him when he changed his call to, "Watch out for the mustard!"
3. A small city couldn't get drivers to obey the speed limit until it changed the traffic signs to read, "30 M.P.H. or $65."

Emotional appeal moves mountains. If you want to increase your business, use words that speak to the emotional interests of your readers. Like you, all they really care about is themselves. It's simply a fact of life. Even the most altruistic are giving because of how good it makes them feel. According to a now out-of-print book by Roy Garn, titled *The Magic Power of Emotional Appeal,* there are four paths to tapping into your client's emotions: self-preservation, romance, money, and recognition.

1. *Recognition.* A newspaper stand in New York, only fifteen yards away from another stand, rang up four times as many sales as its competitor. How? After every sale the owner said, "Thank you." Customers would go out of their way just to be recognized and thanked.

2. *Money.* When Abraham Lincoln was asked for a credit reference, he wrote a letter saying, "Yours of the 10th received. First of all, he has a wife and a baby; together they ought to be worth $500,000 to any man. Second, he has an office in which there is a table worth $1.50 and three chairs worth, say, $1. Last of all, there is in one corner a large rat-hole, which will bear looking into. Respectfully, A. Lincoln." This classic note appealed to the creditors' emotions because it showed the character of the man asking for money.

3. *Self-preservation.* A businessman tried to increase traffic at his store by building a bigger parking lot and putting up signs

saying "Park Here." But nothing happened until he changed the signs to read, "Protected Parking." The new signs helped drivers feel safe, even though there was nothing new about the parking lot. Business boomed.

4. *Romance.* Roy Garn was scheduled to give a talk to women titled, "Emotional Appeal—Key to Happier Living." When he discovered that all the women coming to his lecture were single and actively shopping for men (this was in the 1950s), he changed his title and packed the house. The new title? "How to Use Emotional Appeal—and Get a Husband!"

How do you apply these insights to your online ads? The rule of thumb may be to always address what interests your clients, not you. As I know I've said before, my advice to anyone who wants to write persuasive copy is to "Get out of your ego and into your reader's ego."

Write your ad in a way that helps readers envision themselves with your product or service. Paint a vivid picture of how wonderful their life will be once they have your product. Dramatize the benefits. The more you can help the readers feel, the closer they will come to buying from you. Why? Because an unspoken truth in marketing is that *people do things only for the good feelings they get.* If there aren't any good feelings in your product or service, it's unlikely anyone will pay attention to your offer. In your ad, let readers know what those good feelings are. Write your copy so that they can see, hear, touch, and taste your product or service. In short, involve them emotionally.

Here's a tip: Studies have shown that the following are common "power words" that get results: *you, your, how, new, who, money, now, people, want,* and *why.* Also, *announcing, guaranteed, revealing, breakthrough, exciting, first, exclusive, free, improved, introducing, love,* and *powerful.* Weave them into your ads to make your writing more personal, involving, and direct.

And here are examples of emotionally rich cybercopy. Notice how the copy dramatizes the benefits:

- "The computer comes with a 20-foot extension cord" sounds meaningless; "The computer comes with a 20-foot extension cord so that you can plug it in anywhere and use it anywhere—even outside by the pool!" conveys excitement.

- "I have a lot of experience as a copywriter" sounds ho-hum; "My twenty years' experience as a direct-mail copywriter will help you gain the most money from each of your direct-mail campaigns" speaks to what interests the client.

- "Our sandwiches are big" sounds like something any bragging chef can say; "Our sandwiches are so big that they may not fit in your car, so you'd better let us deliver them to you" sounds dramatic and unforgettable.

"G" Means *Guarantee* What You Sell

The "G" stands for *guarantee*. You are probably well aware of your own skepticism when reading ads, whether online or in the newspaper. People need to know that they are not going to be gypped. Guarantee your services, and say so in your post.

This doesn't have to be elaborate, but it does need to be there. The wisest advice I can give you here is to make your guarantee a "risk reversal." Instead of the customer taking all the risk by buying your service, put all the risk on you. Spell out a guarantee that no sane person could resist. "Guaranteed for ten days" puts all the risk on the customer; "Guaranteed for life" puts all the risk on you. If you want more sales, lighten the risk for your potential clients. After all, if you truly believe that your product or service is tops, why not guarantee it?

Don't worry about people taking advantage of you. Studies show that fewer than 2 percent of your customers will ever ask for their money back. Having a praiseworthy guarantee makes it easier for them to buy, yet barely influences whether they will ever ask for their money back or not. If you want results, add a guarantee that can't be beat.

"E" Means Offer *Evidence*

Gary Blake and Robert W. Bly, in their book *The Elements of Business Writing*, state: "Use facts, opinions, and statistics to prove

your case. Do not expect readers to readily accept every statement you make as the truth. Many people are skeptical; most
will want proof."

The "E" in our TARGET formula stands for *evidence*. Prove
your claims. Give testimonials from satisfied customers. I don't
think there's anything more powerful than reading short quotes
from other people about your business. I don't even need to recognize any of those people to believe them. Just seeing testimonials seems to convey an aura of honesty.

Ask your current clients for endorsements. When they
spontaneously praise your service, ask whether you can have
their statement in writing. The more testimonials you can
gather, the better. Add these quotes to your ad. Let your own
customers do your selling.

Here are a few tips on making your endorsements more
persuasive:

1. *Don't rewrite them*. The more the quote sounds real, even
if it happens to violate rules of good English, the better. You
don't want the quotes to sound as if an advertising wizard wrote
them. Let real people speak in their own idiosyncratic ways.

2. *Add the full name*. Don't use initials as a credit. Saying
"J.T." likes your service means nothing because "J.T." sounds
fictional. Use real names. (And always get permission first.)

3. *Be concrete*. The more specific the quote, the better for
you. "He helped me" isn't anywhere near as believable as "His
feed helped me raise twelve more chickens than last month."

But your evidence can take other forms. Facts and statistics
can be very persuasive. Include whatever you have that is relevant to your case. Don't overdo the evidence, but certainly share
it if you have it. Assume that your readers won't believe your
claims. Find evidence to support what you say, and give it.

"T" Means *Tell* Them What to Do

Tell is the final "T" in TARGET. End your e-ad with a call to
action. Tell your reader to write, call, visit, or e-mail you. And

make it easy to do so. Asking someone to "write back" sounds like work; asking them to "jot something down" sounds easy. Requesting that people fill out a form isn't as easy as asking them to pick up the phone; asking them to visit you isn't as easy as saying you will visit them. Make responding a snap.

Far too many ads, if they manage to get this far in the formula, forget to ask the reader to do anything. This is like walking into a store and having the salespeople just look at you. Wouldn't you prefer them to offer to help, or to show you around, or to ask whether you want socks with those new shoes? Ads that don't have a sales close are incomplete ads. Even if you are practicing the famous "two-step" approach, where you run a teaser ad in order to get people to ask you for more information, you want people to contact you for that further information. Say so.

Another unspoken general truth in marketing is that people like to be led. Don't leave their action up to them. You may not see any action that way. Tell your readers what to do. Spell it out. "Call me at _____ for more details," or "Reply by e-mail and we'll send you the full report," or "Just pick up your fax and. . . ."

Tell them what to do, or don't expect action. This is akin to many poor ads that simply show a picture of a product and give no further information. It would be like walking into a store and having a salesperson walk up and silently hold a product in front of you. It would seem pretty strange, wouldn't it? Don't let your ads become oddities.

Recently I saw an ad for a screen saver by Sony. I was intrigued by the product and wanted it. But the ad didn't tell me how to buy it. I was eager, money in hand, ready to buy, but the copywriter neglected to give me the details on how to order. A toll-free number would have been enough, or even an e-mail address. None of that was there. Without a close, or a call to action, your ad won't bring the sales you want.

Renew Your Ads

Unless your ad is on a website, you will need to renew it continuously by reposting it. The nature of the online world is such that new ads are being posted around the clock, meaning that your ad is being buried under new ads every moment. The only way to come close to remaining current is by reposting your ad. A good rule of thumb is to repost your ads every three weeks. And if you're on America Online, it wouldn't hurt to post your ad early in the day, hoping that it will seem fresh to users as they log on throughout the day.

Having to repost your ads shouldn't seem too odd. In the real world you have to renew your ads to keep them running. Whether you have a television spot or a classified ad in your local newspaper, you must keep your ads current. The same policy is true online.

Hire the Right CyberCopywriter

Copywriting is a skill and a profession just like any other professional service. You may not want to write your ads yourself. If that is the case, what do you do?

Unfortunately, far too many people are claiming to be copywriters when they have no skill, experience, or education in the profession. So far there does not exist a licensing service or even a complete educational program to train someone to be an adept copywriter. This means anyone with the inclination can hang a shingle on the door, print a business card, or even write and post an ad claiming to be a copywriter.

A client of mine in Nashville said he was amazed to find that most of the copywriters he met had never read a book on copywriting. Many of the "copywriters" I've met have a wooden, sophisticated, anticopy style of writing. Advertising legend David Ogilvy says one of the "bees in his bonnet" is the fact that nearly all copywriters have never read any of the classic books on copywriting, such as *Confessions of an Advertising Man* by Ogilvy, *Scientific Advertising* by Claude Hopkins, *How to Write a Good Advertisement* by Victor Schwab, or any of the masterpieces by John Caples.

Most copywriters don't know that copywriting is selling with words. Just because someone can write a newspaper story or a novel does not mean that he or she can write copy that sells.

Be very careful when considering hiring a copywriter. Keep the following in mind:

1. *Ask for references.* Does the copywriter have an impressive list of satisfied clients and a large collection of testimonials?
2. *Ask for credentials.* Why does this person claim to be a copywriter?
3. *Ask to see some of the copywriter's work.* Has she or he written ads, or just articles and stories? Did the ads get results?
4. *Ask how the copywriter was trained.* Did he or she study at a university, work at an ad agency, or take a special program? Or was she or he self-taught?
5. *Has the person previously written ads for the online world?* Did the ads get results?

Test Your Ads

I often show my associates the ads that I write. I'll watch them as they read. If they finish and look at me and say, "Well done," I know I failed. But if they finish reading, look at me, and say, "How can I get this product?" then I know I have a winner. (Of course I'm assuming that they are at least interested in what the product can do for them. If they aren't in my target market, I wouldn't expect them to be interested.)

A successful ad should lead to sales, not peer approval. Many of the ads that people think are funny or creative or well written don't sell a thing. Be sure your ads do what you want. Let others, preferably people in your target market, read them. One of my favorite questions to ask someone who is reviewing one of my ads is, "Would you buy the product or service?" If not, why not? What did I forget to say in the ad?

One of the wonderful benefits of doing business online is the idea that you can easily test ads and get immediate feedback. Write a headline and post it. Note how many replies you get. Write another headline and post it. Did you get more, or fewer, replies? The feedback is instantaneous. Once you have an ad that gets noticed and gets people to act, post it everywhere that seems appropriate and add it to your website. Let it stay online and continue to pull in business for you.

Figure 7–1 is an example of an excellent cyberad.

Summary

"In this complex age, economy of the reader's time must be considered in wording an advertisement." Those words were written by Herbert F. de Bower in *Advertising Principles* in 1918—

Figure 7-1

```
OUR FEATURED PUBLICATION
''Instant Guts! How to Take Intelligent Risks in Every
Area of Your Life'' by Joan Gale Frank
    Do you ever feel like a hamster on a wheel? Do you
secretly know you can do better? Then you need ''Instant
Guts!'' Apply to ears to promote courage and increase
your willingness to take risks in business,
creativity, relationships and adventure. Recommended
for use while driving moving vehicles.
    Will *NOT* cause drowsiness. In seventy minutes you
will know how to identify the best risks for you, the ten
major obstacles to risk-taking and how to overcome
them, how to make fear and mistakes work for you, and the
exact steps to take to make risk-taking easy.
    Dr. Wayne Dyer says, ''Instant Guts! is a great tape
for helping you to overcome your inertia and get your
life on purpose.''
            $10.95 audiotape, plus shipping 70 minutes
                    ISBN 1-882940-00-8
                    ORDERING INFORMATION:
To order, call 1-800-852-4890, or send $12.95 shipping
included, to:
95 Red Rock Way #M108, San Francisco, California 94131
            Send e-mail instntguts@aol.com
```

decades before computers were even invented. Yet his statement holds true today. People are busy. Get to the point in your ads—fast.

One way to streamline your message is to pretend you have a potential customer in front of you. What would you say? Many people often become wordy bores when they sit at the keyboard. A way to cut through the clutter is to mentally converse with one prospect. If you knew that Mary Glenn liked boating, you would know that she would be a prospect for an ad about a boat for sale. And if you called Mary Glenn on the phone and wanted to sell her the boat, wouldn't you be friendly but direct? Wouldn't you say something along the lines of, "Mary, I know you love fishing. I have a boat that I'm no longer using. It's three years old and needs a paint job, but I think it's so good you can take it anywhere and fill it with fish. Would you like to see it?"

As Shakespeare wrote, "An honest tale speeds best being plainly told."

8

How to Turbocharge Your CyberWriting

This may be *the* most important chapter in this *entire* book!

Have I got your attention?

Good. That was the plan. Now ask yourself why I have your attention. What grabbed you? What made you want to keep reading? How come you're reading even now? Let me take a guess:

First, I hit you—hard!—with a simple but solid statement.

Second, I made the line stand out by leaving it as a solitary first sentence.

Third, I gave the line greater impact by italicizing some of the words.

That's almost a formula for creating hypnotic cyberwriting. Almost but not quite. Hypnotic cyberwriting requires relentless fine-tuning. You have to fidget with words and phrases and sentences until each line kills. Every line has to work to keep the reader sucked in and reading on.

How do you create writing of this caliber? You have to follow the basic "Turbocharge Your Writing" formula, which is write first, edit last. First you get a rough draft down. Then you go back and edit it to perfection. A friend of mine, a sculptor, does something similar when he first sketches out his idea, then works to bring it into living form. And as E. B. White said, "There is no great writing, only great rewriting."

Since most people create wimpy writing, online or off, you can make your cyberwriting leap way past the competition and jump off the computer screen by learning how to *activate* your sentences. Most people online write passively. They have no idea how to pump action into their sentences. Yet when you write in a more "turbocharged" fashion, you will create e-text that rivets people to the screen and clearly communicates and persuades.

You create hypnotic cyberwriting of this caliber in the rewriting stage. First you sit down at your computer and write a first draft. You pretend you are sitting in front of the person you want to communicate with, and you "speak" at the keyboard; you type what you would say in person. You then take what you have and you whittle it—sculpt it—polish it—to perfection. Let me show you what I do with a few specific examples:

The door was opened by Joe.

Say that's a line in an article you're working on. It's not bad, but it isn't good, either. It's too passive. A minor tinkering can help this line out.

Joe opened the door.

Getting better, isn't it? Now we have someone doing something. That's active and much more involving. There's life in the sentence now. But is it hypnotic? Nope. So let's try again:

Joe kicked open the door.

That would grab your attention, wouldn't it? But I think we can do better.

Joe KICKED open the door!

Expressed online it would read "Joe *kicked* open the door!" Any way you look at it, now we have an irresistible line. Start your message with that one and your reader is bound to go on to the next one.

Every line has to work to keep your reader's attention. The radio is calling, the television is calling, the phone is ringing, the sun is shining, the refrigerator has food in it, there's a new movie at the theater—your lines have to keep your reader nailed to the screen or you'll lose him or her to any or all of the above.

There are simply too many distractions in the world for you to offer mediocre writing. You don't have a choice. You must rewrite your material to perfection. You *must*!

Years ago I wrote a sales letter to offer a program called Thoughtline. Because my money was riding on the success of that letter, I needed it to work. If you come to your writing with the same attitude, that you must win, that your whole career is riding on this, then you will make it work. I wanted Thoughtline to be a hit. But not a small hit. I wanted a *big, amazing, unforgettable, incredible, make-me-laugh-all-the-way-to-the-bank* hit. I got it, too. But I had to rewrite the sales letter a hundred times. Let me give you a taste of what I did. At one point in the original letter I said the following:

I was impressed when I used Thoughtline the first time.

Garbage! Who cares? So I rewrote the line to make it knock people off their chairs:

The first time I used Thoughtline, it developed an outline for me that made my eyes pop!

Notice the difference? I watched people as they read this new line, and when they came across the words "eyes pop," their eyes would widen—almost as if they were popping open. Clearly a hypnotic line.

Here's another example: A client of mine was working on a new book. She was having trouble developing copy for the back cover, so she called me for some advice. I told her, "Make every line *active* and *personal* and *alive!*"

She didn't understand. We set up a meeting for a consultation so that I could walk her through the process. I went to her and we began talking.

"What do you want to say about your book?" I asked.

"It'll educate people about networking."

"How?" I inquired.

"By teaching them to use themselves resourcefully."

"Give me a specific tip."

"We say you are only four or five people away from anyone

in the world," she explained. "If you use your network, you can meet anyone."

"Great! We'll use that for starters," I said. And on a sheet of paper I wrote the following:

You can reach anyone in the world through networking.

Then I looked at my client and told her what I was going to do.

"That line is bland," I told her. "Let's change it into a question and see if it's more intriguing."

I wrote the following.

Did you know you are only four or five people
away from anyone you want to meet in the world?

Better, I thought to myself, but no cigar. I wrote another line down under it:

Whom do you need to see to get what you want?

Still not good enough. My client observed it all with mounting excitement.

Did you know you are only four or five people away from
presidents, celebrities, millionaires, and royalty?

Not bad!

"That's good!" my client said, smiling.

"It is," I admitted. "But we can do better. If you push past the obvious ideas, something deeper, and usually better, will come up."

"How do you make it better than that?" she asked.

"You can always make it better," I said. "One thing you can do is keep playing with the line until something triggers a breakthrough for you."

"That sounds like work to me."

"It is, it is," I agreed. "But it's an exhilarating challenge once you realize you are creating lines that actually influence people! They'll buy your ideas or products on the strength of what you write down. It's worth the extra work."

I'm not sure whether she bought my argument or not, but I still stand behind my words.

If you want to create writing that nails your readers to the page, work at it. One of the biggest problems with online writing is people's tendency to dash off a message without thinking about what they want to say, let alone rewriting the text so that it has nuclear power. Again, all great writing comes from thoughtful rewriting.

My client and I again looked at her new line. I stared at her for a moment, waiting for my unconscious to say something. I didn't have to wait long. I wrote:

> *"You are only four people away from meeting* millionaires, celebrities, *or* greatness! *Who are those four people? Your* friends!"

Getting better. We stopped there, but you can see how the process works. You keep trying ideas until something connects. Rewriting is the secret here. You rewrite and rewrite—always working to make your lines riveting—and you don't stop until you've succeeded.

How to Make Your CyberWriting Walk, Talk, and Breathe!

Now here are some ways to help you perfect, polish, and strengthen your writing. Apply these tools and you'll create on-line writing that walks, talks, and breathes!

First Way: Use a Thesaurus

Obvious, isn't it? You've probably used a thesaurus at one time or another. Most writers use it for the wrong reasons, however. A still active myth is that writing has to be "intellectual." Victims of this myth use a thesaurus to change simple words into complex ones. Wrong! Use your thesaurus to make your writing simple and direct. If you have a long word, hunt down a shorter one. Mark Twain said he got paid the same amount whether he used the word "policeman" or "cop." Since Twain was lazy, "cop" was easier to use—and quicker. You should follow the same pattern. Find short words that say what you mean. Delete the long words. People trip over them.

Here's a rule of thumb: If you don't use the word in normal conversation, don't use it in your writing. Said another way: If you haven't heard the word at the airport or at a bus stop, don't use it. You should also use your thesaurus when you need a different word to say what you've already said. In other words, if you've been using the word "simple" several times in an article, find another word that says the same thing. Keep your writing fresh and your readers interested by finding clean, easily understood words to express your thoughts. Since I have an on-line thesaurus, I'll use it right now to find another word for "simple." As it turns out, there are a couple of dozen synonyms for "simple." Even I was surprised! Here are a few words from the alternatives:

clear	*natural*
intelligible	*neat*
lucid	*plain*
understandable	*unadorned*
unmistakable	*unaffected*

And the list goes on.

Here's what I would do with this list: I'd scan it and look at all the short words that would fit in my writing. I'd skip words like "understandable." Even though it is simple, I want the most direct word I can find. "Understandable" has too many syllables. "Neat" and "plain" are good bets because they are only one syllable. "Lucid" sounds as if it would work, but I'm not sure everyone understands what it means. For that reason, I'd skip it. You always want to use words that don't have misleading meanings.

A thesaurus is a handy tool to have at your side (or on your computer) because it gives you options. When you need a simple word to replace a long or complicated one, open your thesaurus. When you need to find a word to replace an overused one, use your thesaurus. It's a simple (there's that word again) but powerful way to turbocharge your cyberwriting.

Second Way: Use a Simile Book

Falser Than a Weeping Crocodile and Other Similes by Elyse and Mike Sommer (Detroit: Visible Ink, 1991) should also go on your shelf. I don't always find it inspiring, but using it is as compelling as a gun at your head. Thumb through it to find colorful phrases to clarify your writing.

A simile, by the way, is a phrase used to compare two different ideas. When I said the book was "as compelling as a gun at your head," I was using a simile.

A simile can give your readers a nice jolt. They are reading along and suddenly you make a comparison that surprises them. That's electrifying. If you say a man's smile was like a slit in the sidewalk, you used a simile and you gave your readers an image they can see.

When you use similes, you can make your words

fall softly as rose petals
or gush out like toothpaste
or sting and creep like insects!

Get the idea?

What about my client and her book on networking? How could she use similes to improve her writing?

There isn't a heading called "Networking" in the simile book I have, but there is one called "Friendship." One simile we might use is, "Life without a friend is like life without sun." Maybe my client could say, "Networking is as important to your life as sunshine."

Another simile in the book is, "Without a friend the world is a wilderness." My client might say something like, "Without learning how to network, the world is a wilderness."

Using similes isn't always easy for me. Browsing through the collection and wondering how I can use these similes feels like swimming upstream in chocolate pudding. It's not at all like making instant coffee. (Notice the two similes?) The effort is worth it, however. All the paragraphs in this section were written with the help of my simile book. I feel that my writing is better with similes. And probably clearer. Even though writing with similes sometimes feels like playing the piano with boxing gloves, I have to admit that a good simile is like a loving kiss on a dark rainy day. It's nice.

Warning: Don't overuse similes. They are handy for putting some brightness in your writing, but if you overdo it, your readers will overdose and pass out. They will mentally fog over and no further thoughts will get through.

Spice up your online text with a good simile and your writing will sell like cold lemonade at a marathon. Overdo it and your writing will read like a bad advertisement for jelly. Got the picture?

Third Way: Use a Book of Analogies

"Become a writing *wizard!* Turn your words into *spells* no mortal can resist!"

Those two lines were inspired by a brief glance in another book you need on your shelf: *The Analogy Book of Related Words* by Selma Glasser (Buena Vista, Colo.: Communication Creativity, 1990).

The book is billed as "Your Secret Shortcut to Power Writing." I'm not sure whether that's true, but the book can certainly tickle your mind into creating juicy new phrases. Glasser's book is a word-storming partner. Just open it to one of the several lists, all sorted by categories, and let your mind connect the words listed with the ideas you're trying to get across.

I was thinking of advertising a writing manual I wrote when I opened her book to the category called "Myth and Legend." I saw the word "wizard" and the word "spell" and I was suddenly inspired to write the line that began this section. Here's a demonstration of how the book works: Let's say I want to add spice to my client's book on networking. I open Glasser's book to *any* category. It fell open to "Baseball," and now I let my eyes roam the lists of related words. There's "bag, ball, club, error, all-star, fastball," and a bunch more words. And then it happened! Lightning struck and—*aha!*—my mind made a new connection:

> *Don't strike out! Become a business all-star with these fast-ball concepts!*

See how it works?

Here's one more quick example: I'm thinking of how I can describe this manual as I open Glasser's book to the category of "Chess." Over a hundred words are listed. Without more than a glance at the list I immediately have a new line:

> *The strategies in this manual will teach you how to check-mate the competition!*

I could go on and on (and maybe I have). Use Glasser's book to alter mediocre lines into sentences that tap-dance and sing. You don't want to change every line into a new phrase, but doing it now and then adds incredible color to your writing.

Fourth Way: Use a Book of Quotes

John F. Kennedy once said, "Let us resolve to be masters, not the victims, of our history, controlling our own destiny without giving way to blind suspicions and emotions."

What does that quote have to do with turbocharging your cyberwriting? Nothing. But it sure looks good on the page, doesn't it? That's the first reason to use quotes: They are visually appealing. Readers want to see quotation marks in your writing. They want dialogue because dialogue brings text to life. Using quotes is one way to get dialogue (or what looks like dialogue) into your writing.

All the books of quotations I see at the bookstores are evidence that people love quotes. They are short, usually wise, often witty, and usually said by someone we all know (like Kennedy). The goal for you and me is to find quotes that add drama to our writing. Here's an example: When I was working on my Thoughtline sales letter, I kept thumbing through books of quotations. One of my favorites is called *The Wit and Wisdom of Mark*

Twain (Alex Ayres, ed. New York: New American Library, 1987). As I was flipping through its pages, my eyes caught sight of this quote: "A man's intellect is stored powder; it cannot touch itself off; the fire must come from outside."

A light bulb flashed over my head (my cats saw it) and I knew that was the quote to include in my sales letter. So I used Twain's quote, added a line to make it even more relevant to my readers, and put it all in a box to make it stand out. The result was this:

Mark Twain wrote, "A man's intellect is stored powder; it cannot touch itself off; the fire must come from outside." Thoughtline is the "fire" you need to make your mind EX-PLODE!

Catches your eye, doesn't it?

Quotes add spice to your writing. Glance at any letter and if there's a quote, your eyes will spot it instantly. Quotes add aliveness, too, because they are perceived as living. Again, that's because people associate anything in quotations with dialogue, and dialogue is considered to be happening in real time (here and now). It's difficult to pass up anything with quotations in it.

Your quotes can't be very long, of course. Even quotation marks won't save you if your quote runs several lines long. Again, you want to be short and sweet. Mark Twain's quote has a couple of breaks in it, but it is essentially only one line.

Your goal in selecting quotes is to find one that is:

1. *Short* (one line is best)
2. *Relevant* (ties in with your point)
3. *From someone most of your readers will recognize* (a celebrity or authority, like Twain or Kennedy)

Pavlov, the Russian scientist, said, "Men are apt to be much more influenced by words than by the actual facts of the surrounding reality."

Words have power. Words in a good quote can be powerful

enough to alter the world. Whoever said the pen is mightier than the sword wasn't lying.

There are many good books of quotations available in the reference section of your favorite bookstore to help you in locating golden one-liners. Buy several and put them on the shelf along with your thesaurus and book of similes. They are all strong tools to help you create irresistible turbocharged cyberwriting.

Twelve CyberCopywriting Tips

As stated earlier, text rules online, but most people have no idea how to write it effectively. As you surf cyberspace, keep the following essential tips in mind:

1. *Activate your writing*. Whenever you write the words "is," "was," "are," or "to be," train yourself to stop and change them to something more active. "The meeting *is* tonight" sounds dead; "The meeting *starts* at 7:00 P.M. sharp tonight" feels clear, direct, and alive. "Clair Sullivan is the finest promoter in the country" doesn't convey the excitement that "Clair Sullivan creates corporate events better than anyone else on the planet" does.

2. *Be specific*. Whenever you write something vague, such as "they say," or "later on," or "many," train yourself to stop and rewrite those phrases into something more concrete, such as: "Mark Weisser said . . . " or "Saturday at noon" or "Seven people agreed." Don't say "dog" when you can say "collie."

3. *Add excitement*. Use the various books we discussed, whether a quote book, thesaurus, or book of analogies, to add emotional richness to your writing. That way you can make your cyberwriting stand out like a giraffe at a billy goat convention.

4. *Involve readers*. Cyberspace is interactive. Quiz readers. Question them. Tease them. Involve them. The more you can bring readers into a relationship with your text, the better.

5. *Focus on benefits*. Features are technical details; benefits are what we get from having those technical details. If a micro-

wave popper holds a gallon of popcorn, that's a feature; being able to pop enough corn to easily feed a hungry family and their guests is a benefit. A common mistake is assuming everyone knows what you are talking about when you state a technical fact. Computer magazine advertisers still haven't learned that the vast majority of people looking at their ads don't understand all the technical mumbo-jumbo they list. Saying a modem is a 28.8 is not a benefit most people can relate to. But if you say, "A 28.8 modem will allow you to see graphics within seconds as opposed to minutes, so you don't waste any time staring at your monitor," you've stated a benefit people understand.

6. *Be human*. Write conversationally. Again, forget impressing people with large words or complex sentences. Be real. Say what you have to say and stop. Pretend you are speaking to one person. And although you want to proofread your work, don't focus so much on being grammatically correct. Your English teacher won't be grading your cyberwriting, and your English teacher probably never sold anything, anyway. Write to communicate, not to impress.

7. *Forget graphics*. At least don't rely on them. Less than 15 percent of the online population has the means to see graphics. The rest may be using slow modems, which means sitting around and waiting for the graphics to download. Nearly all the selling will be done by your words, not your graphics. Focus on your text.

8. *Remember how you look*. Keep your text narrow, about four to six inches (or about forty characters) wide. Use short, single-spaced paragraphs, and add a space between them. If your on-line text looks dense, people will skip it. Make it visually inviting.

9. *Deliver one message*. One main idea per screen or per message works best. If you have more to say, consider printing a hard copy and snail-mailing it to your readers. Reading pages of online text can cause eyestrain. Most e-messages should be treated as if they were slightly long telegrams or short business letters. Get to your point. Fast.

10. *Remember that emotion sells*. People buy for emotional reasons and justify their decision with logic. Always speak in

emotional terms. Tell a story. Give testimonials. Use words that convey feeling. Help people imagine using or having your product or service. Paint a picture they can see as well as feel. Dramatize your benefits. Be colloquial.

When I posted a message about the results of a survey on signature files, I could have written, "People here were upset about my post." But that sounds lame. I added emotion by being more colloquial. I wrote, "Several of you replied to my post, some of you so angry that you wanted to eat the skin off my back."

One person saw my post and said, "I may not agree with what you said, but I'll never forget how you said it."

11. *Avoid sexist language.* You could get flamed big-time by sounding sexist online. Instead of writing such words as "chairman," "coed," or "fireman," replace them with such words as "chairperson," "student," or "firefighter." Remember, we no longer have "mailmen"; we now have "mail carriers." We no longer have "workmen"; we now have "workers."

12. *Remember the globe.* Your cyberwriting will be read by users across the planet. When you list your address, add your country. When you give your phone number, add your international dialing prefix. When you give ordering information, be sure to mention the fee for overseas shipping. You're no longer writing for the local newspaper, but for the entire globe. Keep the citizens of Earth in mind.

CyberMarketing 101

Keep two basic facts in mind when writing online copy for web pages, Usenet posts, catalogs, or ads:

1. *People do not care about you or your business until you show them how you can help them.* Far too many businesses create a website and write online copy that explains who they are. No one cares! People simply want to know, "What's in it for me?"

2. *People universally feel deprived.* Unconscious or not, there

is a quiet desperation within each of us. Focus on how your business alleviates this feeling.

In other words, nearly all of us feel that we are lacking in appearances, wealth, health, romance, safety, or happiness. While focusing on the positive (few people like to be reminded of anything negative), clearly show how your business helps people in any of those areas, and they will probably do business with you. Instead of reminding people that they don't have much money, show them how they can have more money; instead of reminding people that they aren't as attractive as they could be, show them how they can be more attractive. Focus on the positive, on how your service can heal their pain.

Summary

Cyberwriting can make or break your business. Spend time writing posts that focus on benefits to your customers. Remember that the most famous definition of advertising—"advertising is salesmanship in print"—still helps define advertising online. The medium may be different, but the purpose and the people are very much the same. If your writing is active, involving, and personal, your selling results should be impressive.

9

The "Drip System" of CyberSpace

At the end of the preceding chapter I mentioned two basic facts about marketing: People do not care about you or your business until you show them how you can help them, and people universally feel deprived. Another fundamental truth in marketing, online or not, is that *people are lonely and want to be loved.* This can be profitable news for you. This chapter will show you why.

Treat Them Like Dogs!

Years ago I wrote a special report on service titled "Treat Them Like Dogs: The Easiest Way to Keep Customers Forever!" The message was that we treat our pets better than we do our clients. Yet if we don't take care of our customers, they won't take care of us. As numerous studies have shown, one of the key reasons customers stop doing business with us is indifference on the part of the business. And to add salt to this wound, other studies show that an unhappy customer will broadcast his or her unhappiness about the business to an average of eight other people. That's the dark side of networking.

People want to be recognized, appreciated, and respected. Give them that sense of love and they will stay loyal to you. My special report urged people to start pampering customers. What would happen if you truly "watered, walked, stroked, and fussed over" your customers just as most people do with their pets? At first your customers would be surprised. But they would soon learn to love it. And they would quickly tell others about your phenomenal service. That's free advertising for you.

Being online gives you an opportunity to show recognition and appreciation of your customers. All you have to do is create what netties call an e-zine, or electronic magazine or newsletter, and then "drip" it to your database.

The Drip System

Marketing professionals know that the drip system keeps customers and clients happy. When you stay in contact with your past customers on a regular and consistent basis, you are implementing the drip system. When a faucet leaks, the drip gets attention. In the offline world, that "drip" can be anything from a postcard to a letter to a newsletter to anything else you can imagine. Online, one of the best ways to "drip" something to your database of clients is with an e-zine.

E-zines are the electronic equivalent of company newsletters or even special-interest magazines. They are topic-specific online magazines. If you create an e-zine that interests your customers and clients, you create a way for them to remember you while helping them feel that you care about them.

For a fairly complete listing of available e-zines, check out **http://www.meer.net/~johnl/e-zine-list/index.html**. You will also find resources on how to create and promote your own e-zine at that site.

Here are a few examples of e-zines:

- *Wall Street News.* This e-zine delivers information on stocks.

Send e-mail to:	*Wall-Street-News-request@netcom.com*
Subject:	Ignored
Body:	subscribe Wall-Street-News

- *The Contrarian Advisor.* This one focuses on out-of-favor stocks.

Send e-mail to:	*choyt@Interactive.net*
Subject:	Subscribe Contrarian
Body:	send your e-zine please

- *Internet Business Journal.* This one delivers information about business in cyberspace.

Send e-mail to:	*listserv@poniecki.berkeley.edu*
Subject:	None
Body:	SUB IBJ-L [*your name*]

Think of Your Clients

A vast majority of the e-zines available online are computer-oriented, mainly because the vast majority of people online are computer-savvy. Imagine the people who do business with you. What are they interested in? What do they pay you for? Anyone interested in Wall Street and stocks might be interested in the two e-zines mentioned earlier. If you are a stockbroker, creating an e-zine similar to those might make sense. But assume you're a dentist, or a florist. An e-zine for dental patients might include articles on the best way to prevent cavities; an e-zine from a florist might have articles reminding people of special holidays, or tips on what flowers to send if you're trying to woo a special person.

In short, make your e-zine of interest to your customers, and not necessarily of interest to you. Far too many business people, online or not, create newsletters that are simply long advertisements. If you want people to read your words and think of you when it's time to do business again, give them reading material that genuinely interests them. Again, if you're thinking of your customers and wanting to show your appreciation for them, the only material you can logically deliver is what *they* want to read.

Using Listservs to Net Publicity

Zines can take many forms. One of the most popular for business use is called a **listserv**, which is simply a newsletter that people subscribe to much as they would an e-mailing list. The difference here is that people cannot reply to the list or to anyone on it; they can only receive what you send them. John Martin, a Houston publicist, says listservs are a marketing opportunity for anyone in business. "If you create a zine or a newsletter that excites people," Martin said, "within weeks hundreds to thousands of people will subscribe to it. Think of the free publicity you'll be getting."

Free is right. Listservs do not cost anything to run, other than your monthly maintenance fee. There are usually no subscription fees, usages fees, or online charges. Subscribers to your listserv simply send an e-mail message asking to receive your zine or newsletter. From that point they, and everyone else already on the list, automatically receive whatever you write and approve to send out. In short, you are serving the list with your information, hence the name "listserv."

Your messages can be sent daily, weekly, monthly, or whenever you feel like it (though consistency is best if you want to create an online presence) As with every other written form online, you'll gain greater friendly publicity for your business if your messages are 95 percent useful information and 5 percent sales copy.

Examples of popular listservs are:

- "Wake-Up, Brain!" a weekly stimulating message about creativity and problem solving that also plugs books, software, and other tools.

  Send e-mail to: majordomo@thinksmart.com
  Subject: None
  Message: subscribe wake-up, brain

- "EDUPAGE" delivers fascinating information to help educate you about online-related activities.

  Send e-mail to: listproc@educom.unc.edu
  Subject: None
  Message: subscribe edupage [*your name*]

- "National Lawyers Guild Electronic Mailing List" delivers information from and to attorneys.

Send e-mail to: *listserv@ubvm.cc.buffalo.edu*
Subject: None
Message: sub LGUILD-L [*your name*]

- "This is True" delights thousands of subscribers every week when Randy Cassingham's bizarre but true stories from the world's press arrives by e-mail. He was easily able to sell his book, *This is True: Deputy Kills Man With Hammer* (Pasadena, Cal.: Freelance Publications, 1995), to his subscribers by simply mentioning its availability at the end of his weekly message.

Send e-mail to: *listserv@netcom.com*
Subject: None
Message: subscribe this-is-true

What to Write

As always, whenever you are trying to sell something, think of what's in it for your prospects. Imagine them sitting in front of you. What do they care about? What are their interests and concerns? One way to look at this is to ask, "What is their pain?" Your clients are coming to you to get relief from something. What is it? How does your business help cure what ails your customers?

Your answers will help direct you to what to write. If you are an accountant, a weekly or monthly online newsletter about "How to Save Taxes" or "Five Tips on Saving Money" might be of value. But any practical and interesting information could have the same effect. You want people to eagerly subscribe to, read, and remember your message. If they do, they will also remember you and your services.

One of my clients told me about a marketing coach who sends out weekly e-mail to his subscribers offering tips on achieving goals. "If nothing else," my client reported, "every Monday I am reminded of what he does. One day I will hire him." My client added that he already purchased some of the coach's books and tapes. Those products had been mentioned at the end of the coach's messages.

A proven easy way to write articles is the "Five Steps to . . ." approach. Just imagine wanting to write a short column on how to do something. It doesn't matter what. Now pick a number. Again, it doesn't matter. "Five Steps to Writing a Business Plan" can just as easily become "Nine Steps to Writing a Business Plan" if you discover you have a few extra steps to write about.

Then simply write the piece. You don't have to tell readers everything. Give them enough information so they feel that they learned something. I have written numerous reports on how to write sales letters and press releases. Even the clients who bought and read everything still hire me when they need a letter or release. The articles give people concrete information, but most people won't act on that information. They'll use it to decide whom to hire when they need the work done. If you're the author of a helpful how-to article, you'll probably be the one hired when the reader needs your service.

An Easy Writing Formula

Another tip in writing any article or special report is the "tell them and prove it" formula. State your principle or point and then back it up with three stories, quotes, facts, or statistics. This is an easy way to write anything, from a memo to a book.

Here's how it works:

1. List the points you want to make.
2. For each one, jot down three supporting statements. You've just created an outline for your writing.
3. Now imagine that you are talking to one reader, and explain each point and supporting statement as you write.

For example, my point in the above paragraph is: "The 'tell them and prove it with three points' formula works for all business writing."

Three supporting statements might be:

1. "In journalism school they taught me to tell readers what I'm about to say, say it, and then tell them what I said."

2. "The software program Thoughtline asks you to list your
    main points, then urges you to support each main point
    with evidence of some sort."
3. "People understand groups of threes."

I might then write a few paragraphs using the above like this:

> My journalism professor pounded into my skull
> the idea that people needed help in remembering
> what they read. He advised helping them by first
> telling them what I was about to say in the first
> paragraph, then explaining my message in the next
> paragraphs, and then wrapping it all up in the final
> paragraphs by recapping the message.
>
> Though I thought he oversimplified things at the
> time, I've learned he was right. I often use the
> artificial intelligence program called
> Thoughtline to help me write. I've noticed that
> when it asks me questions about my writing project,
> it always asks, ''What are your main points?'' And
> after I've typed in my answers, it later comes
> around and probes with the question, ''What is your
> evidence for your main points?'' The program never
> fails to corner me on this, and my answers never
> fail to help me write a more persuasive piece.
>
> I know this formula works for another reason,
> too. Last night I was reading a book on psychology
> and was reminded that our wonderful minds can't
> easily retain more than seven pieces of
> information, like a seven-digit phone number. And
> I noticed that even those seven digits get broken
> up to make recall easier, and we often break them up
> into three and four numbers, such as 999-1110. We
> call this chunking.

All three paragraphs grew out of my simple formula, "tell
them and prove it."

How to Set Up a Listserv

Since you are probably now interested in establishing your own listserv, here's the procedure to follow:

1. Pick a short but descriptive name for your list.

2. Decide whether it will be moderated, meaning that someone (probably you) will read each post and decide whether to allow it to be posted. Moderating a list is time-consuming but helps keep the list clean of flames, hype, or anything else you may not want on it. Be warned that if your list catches on and becomes very popular, you may receive hundreds, even thousands, of e-mail submissions to it every day.

3. Contact your local access provider, usually whoever you have handling your website account. Tell that person of your plans.

4. Fill out the questionnaire he or she sends you.

5. Announce your listserv to the "List of Lists" by sending e-mail to *arielle@taronga.com*.

6. Keep the list alive by seeing that interesting messages are contributed to it on a regular basis. Remember, this list is to help remind prospects and customers of your business. You want the messages it delivers to help you look professional. Give some thought to everything you post. Be sure your posts are of value to your readers.

Summary

Having your own listserv is a way to build and maintain a relationship with prospects and past customers. Simply write a regular and consistent article and "drip" it to your prospects and existing clients. Again, a fundamental law in marketing is that *people like to do business with people they know, like, and respect.* By staying in contact with your database with an e-newsletter, you will create and sustain the relationships needed to increase your bottom-line profits. To make your columns relevant, always think of what interests your readers; to make the writing of the columns easy, always remember the "tell them and prove it" formula.

10

What to Do If You're Flamed

Face it. If Dennis the Menace and Bart Simpson are a few of the character types you'll find online, sooner or later you'll get flamed. There may be no way around it. Even CEOs have their dark sides. If you do get flamed, what do you do? Here are a few suggestions.

First Strategy: Delete It Before Reading It

You can often tell from the subject line that the message you are about to see is a flame. If your header says "You fool!" or something even harsher, you might consider deleting the message without even reading it. The sender's headline is a dead giveaway that you're about to walk into fire. Save yourself the trouble. Delete it.

Second Strategy: Apologize

I've found that apologizing for whatever earned me the flame works best. Whether I'm in the right or in the wrong, the person who flamed me has perceived me as being in the wrong, and that's reason enough to apologize. Had I communicated more clearly whatever I posted, I might not have been flamed.

I've also noted that psychologically this approach wins people over more than any other. Since people like to think they are right in their thoughts, my apologizing lets them maintain their status. My apologizing also completely defuses any chance for further flames. No matter what people say to me in their posts, if I reply, "I'm sorry," I've left them no fuel for any more flaming. I may also have won them over to my side, because they often pause and go back to reread my initial post to see whether maybe they made a mistake in how they read it. This approach also pleasantly surprises people. Those who send a flames expect flames in return. If you apologize, you surprise them.

Third Strategy: Forget It

When I first received a few flames, I got red-hot angry. I thought the people flaming me were inconsiderate, shallow-minded, and obviously ignorant. I'd try writing back and explaining my position. I quickly learned that a fundamental truth in human psychology is that *people will defend to the death their belief that they are right.* Once they have stated a position, trying to change it is harder than moving a mountain with a teaspoon. Writing back never got me anywhere, and usually escalated the flame war.

I'd check my mailbox later and there would be another flame. I've learned that it's best to delete the flame and forget it. Simply move on. This method requires being secure enough in your own self-esteem to not need to retaliate with a flame of your own.

Fourth Strategy: Save Them for Fun

Mark Twain and P. T. Barnum used to collect "queer letters" from people who wrote to Barnum with preposterous ideas for businesses. Though he never got around to it, Twain was eventually going to publish the letters as a book. This might be an effective way to defuse the flames you may get. Save them with the idea that maybe someday you'll write a book about them. I should add that you can't legally do this without the flamer's permission, since he or she owns the copyright on the words, but telling yourself you are going to save these amazing flames for some later use might make receiving them easier to tolerate. Heck, it worked for Twain and Barnum.

Fifth Strategy: Remember the Prime Directive of Cyberspace

In the introduction to this book I mentioned a prime directive I invented for cyberspace: "Write in kindness." As the fifth suggestion for how to handle flames, I want to remind you that whatever you choose to do, remember to write in kindness. As long as you soften your heart when about to reply to a flamer, you should naturally reply in a way that will make you, and the person receiving your message, feel good. Flaming just leads to more flaming, and that just leads to more unhappiness on the planet. It continues the "chain of pain." That's not good for you, me, or our businesses. However you choose to respond to a flame, simply stop, take a deep breath, and remember the mantra, "Write in kindness."

Epilogue: Quick Solutions to CyberWriting's Three Biggest Problems

In the introduction I said there were three challenges with writing online. So that you have instant access to the help you may need, here are my quick tips on handling each of those problems.

First Tip: What Looks Good on Paper Rarely Looks Good Online, and Vice Versa

To be sure your messages look the same on your screen as they do on your readers' screens, do this:

1. Keep your margins wide, text thin (about forty characters a line).
2. Don't use graphics in e-mail.
3. If you use graphics on web pages, make them simple and easy to download for even the slowest modems. "Text heavy; graphics light" is a good rule of thumb.
4. If you still use large graphics, add a text statement that says, "Large graphic. Download time: 7 minutes." That way people can choose to skip it if they want.
5. Proofread everything you send at least twice. Then proofread again.

Second Tip: The "Ambiguity of Intention" Makes Accurate Communication Nearly Impossible

Computer screens don't reveal facial clues or body signals that would otherwise help clarify your intended messages. To compensate, do the following:

1. Ask yourself two questions: "Would I say this to his or her face?" and "Will they be glad to read this?"
2. Soften everything you write. Use statements that defuse any potential misunderstanding. "I am sending this to you because you seem interested in this type of service, if you aren't, I apologize," disarms virtually every potential flame.
3. Remember the prime directive of cyberspace: "Write in kindness."
4. Be honest. Don't try to manipulate or mislead readers. They'll see through it.
5. Assume you'll be misunderstood. Rewrite. Rewrite again. Wait a day before sending your message.

Third Tip: Online, Text Rules; If You Can't Write to Communicate, You're Dead

When all is said and done, it's the words on the screen that make your readers buy, reply, or flame you. To get the results you want, do this:

1. Write about what interests your reader, not you. Deliver information.
2. Focus on benefits, not features. Dramatize what you want to sell.
3. *Be interesting.* Give surprising facts. Add relevant quotes. Tell a story.
4. Talk about what your product or service "cures."
5. Get to the point. Deliver one main idea per message.

Appendix

General Resources

Web Page Creators

- Daniel Kehoe at Fortuity Consulting can design an attention-getting website for you. Contact him at 1-800-808-4260. Or e-mail *kehoe@fortuity.com.*
- Dr. Cliff Kurtzman at the Tenagra Corporation provides Internet marketing, public relations, and high traffic website development. Contact him at 1-713-480-6300. Or e-mail *Cliff.Kurtzman@Tenagra.com.*

Software

- Thoughtline, the artificial intelligence non-Windows program that helps you think through and outline any writing project, is available from Experience in Software. Call 1-800-678-7008.
- Floodgate, the program that grabs e-mail addresses from online messages and helps you create a database of prospects, is available from Neil Albala. Call 1-520-322-0838 or e-mail *neil@voters.com.*

CyberCopywriters

There aren't yet too many professional online copywriters. Here are two:

- Alice Horrigan *alice@netcom.com*
- Joe Vitale *mrfire@blkbox.com* or *jgvitale@ix.netcom.com*

Media Contacts

You can send your press releases by e-mail to the following edited list of media contacts. If you want a publication to print
your news release, include your postal address and phone number for verification purposes. Also, please do not use this list to
send a mass mailing to every single listed media outlet. A bicy-
cling magazine is unlikely to be interested in your thoughts on
abortion, no matter how cogent they are, for example. Target
your media blitz. You can find the most current copy of Adam
Gaffin's compiled list online at **http://www.webcom.com/leavitt/
medialist.html.html**.

Daily Newspapers

Anchorage Daily News	*74220.2560@compuserve.com*
Arkansas Democrat-Gazette, Little Rock	*news@arkdg.com*
Boston Globe	
Story Ideas	*news@globe.com*
Circulation Requests	*circulation@globe.com*
Letters to the Editor	*letter@globe.com*
Submissions to "Voxbox" column	*voxbox@globe.com*
Comments on Coverage/Ombudsman	*ombud@globe.com*
"Ask the Globe"	*ask@globe.com*
Thursday Calendar Section	*list@globe.com*
Health & Science Section	*howwhy@globe.com*
Confidential Chat	*chat@globe.com*
City Weekly Section	*ciweek@globe.com*
Real Estate section	*lots@globe.com*
Religion Editor	*religion@globe.com*
Arts Editor	*arts@globe.com*
"Plugged In"	*plugged@globe.com*
Champaign-Urbana (Ill.) News-Gazette	*gazette@prairienet.org*
Chicago Tribune	*tribletter@aol.com*
Chronicle-Telegram, Elyria, Ohio	*macroncl@freenet.lorain.oberlin.edu*
The Columbus (Ohio) Dispatch	*crow@cd.columbus.oh.us*
Letters to the editor	*letters@cd.columbus.oh.us*
Contra Costa County Times, Calif.	
Letters to the editor	*cctletrs@netcom.com*
Corvallis (Ore.) Gazette-Times	*74250.2373@compuserve.com*
Daily Citizen, Washington, D.C.	*ben@essential.org*
Flint (Mich.) Journal	*fj@flintj.com*
Gazeta Wyborcza, Poland	*gawyb@ikp.atm.com.pl*
The Guardian, U.K.	*letters@guardian.co.uk*
"Notes and Queries"	*nandq@guardian.co.uk*

Computer Page	*computerg@guardian.co.uk*
"Online"	*online@guardian.co.uk*
The Independent, U.K.	
Computer Page	*comppage@independent.co.uk*
International Herald-Tribune	*iht@eurokom.ie*
Jerusalem (Israel) Post	*jpost@zeus.datasrv.co.il*
Journal American, Bellevue, Wash.	*Jaedit@aol.com*
Journal Newspapers, D.C. area	*thejournal@aol.com*
The Knoxville (Tenn.) News-Sentinel	
Newsroom	*kns-news@use.usit.net*
Letters	*kns-letters-to-editor@use.usit.net*
Middlesex News, Framingham, Mass.	*Mnews@world.std.com*
Morning Journal, Lorain, Ohio	*mamjornl@freenet.lorain.oberlin.edu*
The Namibian, Windhoek, Namibia	*tom@namibian.com.na*
Norwich (Conn.) Bulletin	*norbull@aol.com*
The Olympian, Olympia, Wash	*olympian@halcyon.com*
Ottawa Citizen, Ottawa, Ont.	*ottawa-citizen@freenet.carleton.ca*
Peoria Journal Star, Peoria, Ill.	*xxnews@heartland.bradley.edu*
Philadelphia Inquirer (Editorial Page)	*editpage@aol.com*
Portland Oregonian	*oreeditors@aol.com*
Prague Post	*100120.361@compuserve.com*
Sacramento Bee	
Letters, op-ed pieces	*sacbedit@netcom.com*
St. Paul (Minn.) Pioneer Press	
Virtual Reality	*vpress@aol.com*St.
St. Petersburg (Fla.) Times	*73174.3344@compuserve.com*
Salt Lake Tribune, Salt Lake City	*the.editors@sltrib.com*
San Diego Union-Tribune	
Bi-weekly Internet column only	*computerlink@sduniontrib.com*
San Francisco Examiner	*sfexaminer@aol.com*
San Jose Mercury-News	*sjmercury@aol.com*
San Mateo (Calif.) Times	*smtimes@crl.com*
Santa Cruz County (Calif.) Sentinel	
Letters to the editor	*sented@cruzio.com*
News desk	*sentcity@cruzio.com*
Seattle Times	
Personal Technology	*ptech@seatimes.com*
Springfield (Mo.) News-Leader	
Letters to the editor	*nleditor@ozarks.sgcl.lib.mo.us*
Press releases	*nlnews@ozarks.sgcl.lib.mo.us*
Sun-Sentinel, Broward County, Fla.	
Grapevine	*vineeditor@aol.com*
Die Tageszeitung, Berlin	*briefe@taz.de*
Tallahassee Democrat	*letters@freenet.fsu.edu*
Toronto Sun ("Page Six")	*pagesix@aol.com*
USA Today	
Letters to the Editor	*usatoday@clark.net*
Vancouver (Wash.) Columbian	*vanpaper@aol.com*
Winnipeg Free Press, Winnipeg, Man.	
News tips	*citydesk@freepress.mb.ca*

Library	*library@freepress.mb.ca*
Letters to the Editor	*letters@freepress.mb.ca*
Computer Columnist	*pihichyn@freepress.mb.ca*
Computer Editor	*minkin@freepress.mb.ca*

Weekly Newspapers

Austin (Texas) Chronicle	*xephyr@bga.com*
Bay Windows, Boston	*baywindo@world.std.com*
CityPages, Minneapolis	*citypages@igc.apc.org.*
City Paper, Philadelphia	*71632.57@compuserve.com*
Eye, Toronto	*eye@io.org*
New York Press	*nyp@echonyc.com*
Palo Alto Weekly, Palo Alto, Calif.	*Paweekly@netcom.com.*
Ridgefield (Conn.) Press	*71052.3315@compuserve.com*
The Stranger, Seattle	*stranger@cyberspace.com*
Innovation	*innovation@delphi.com*
Tico Times, Costa Rica	*ttimes@huracan.cr*
Twin Cities Reader, Minneapolis	*sari23@aol.com*
The Village Voice, New York, N.Y.	*voice@echonyc.com*
Voir, Montreal	*voir@babylon.montreal.qc.ca*
Washington City Paper	*washcp@aol.com*
Weekly Mail & Guardian, Johannesburg, S.A.	*wmail-info@wmail.misanet.org*

College Newspapers

BG News, Bowling Green State U., Ohio	*bgnews@andy.bgsu.edu*
The Bucknellian, Bucknell U.	*bucknellian@bucknell.edu*
Colorado Daily, Boulder, Colo.	*coloradodaily@onenet-bbs.org*
Cornell Daily Sun	*Cornell.Daily.Sun@cornell.edu*
The Daily Northwestern, Evanston, Ill.	*Daily@merle.acns.nwu.edu*
Daily Pennsylvanian, U. of Pa.	*dailypenn@a1.relay.upenn.edu*
Daily Texan, UT-Austin	*texan@utxvms.cc.utexas.edu*
The Daily Universe, Brigham Young Univ.	
Op-ed submissions	*letters@byu.edu*
Gair Rhydd, Cardiff U., Wales	*gairrhydd@cardiff.ac.uk*
JSU Newsletter, Polytechnic U. of N.Y.	*jsu@photon.poly.edu*
Kansas State Collegian, Kansas State U.R	*johnso@ksu.ksu.edu*
Minnesota Daily, U. of Minnesota	*network@edit.mndly.umn.edu.*
The Muse, Memorial U., Newfoundland	*muse@morgan.ucs.mun.ca*
National College U. Magazine	*umag@well.sf.ca.us*
Oxford Student, Oxford U.	*theoxstu@black.ox.ac.uk*
The Peak, Univ. of Guelph, Canada	*peak@uoguelph.ca*
Planet Communications, U. of Toronto	*editor@planet.org*
Redbrick, Univ. of Birmingham, U.K.	*redbrick@bham.ac.uk*
The Reporter, Polytechnic Univ of N.Y.	*reporter@photon.poly.edu*
The Sewanee Purple, U. of the South	*purple@seraph1.sewanee.edu*
The Student Movement, Andrews U., Mich.	*smeditor@andrews.edu*
The Tartan, Carnegie-Mellon U.	*Tartan@andrew.cmu.edu*
The Tech, MIT, Cambridge, Mass.	

Advertising   *ads@the-tech.mit.edu*
Arts   *arts@the-tech.mit.edu*
News   *news@the-tech.mit.edu*
Sports   *sports@the-tech.mit.edu*
Archive management   *archive@the-tech.mit.edu*
Circulation and subscription   *scirc@the-tech.mit.edu*
Free calendar listings   *news-notes@the-tech.mit.edu*
General questions   *general@the-tech.mit.edu*
Letters to the editor   *letters@the-tech.mit.edu*
Photography department   *photo@the-tech.mit.edu*
Cavalier Daily, University of Virginia   *vdaily@virginia.edu*
Washington Square News, NYU   *nyuwsn@aol.com*

Magazines

Advertising Age
   Letters to the editor   *ehbu73a@prodigy.com*
   Interactive Media & Marketing   *gywkj04a@prodigy.com*
Allure   *alluremag@aol.com*
The American Prospect   *tap@world.std.com*
Interface Magazine, Atlanta   *73424.1014@compuserve.com*
Area Magazine, Australia   *pwilken@peg.apc.org*
Brown Alumni Monthly, Providence, R.I.   *bam@brownvm.brown.edu*
Budapest Business Journal, Hungary   *100263.213@compuserve.com*
Business Week   *bwreader@mgh.com*
Chronicle of Higher Education   *editor@chronicle.merit.edu*
Canadian Treasurer, Toronto   *mcdouga@ecf.utoronto.ca*
CAUSE/EFFECT (Submissions Review)   *jrudy@cause.colorado.edu*
Clinical Data Management   *anneb@delphi.com*
Clinical Psychiatry News, Rockville,Md.   *Cpierce@cpcug.org*
Delta (Mathematics, physics, chemistry)   *delta@plearn.edu.pl*
PolandDePauw Magazine, Greencastle, Ind.   *Mlillich@depauw.edu*
Details   *detailsmag@aol.com*
Earth First! Journal   *earthfirst@igc.apc.org*
Family Practice News, Rockville, Md.   *Cpierce@cpcug.org*
Flagship (play by mail) US   *76702.1365@compuserve.com*
Feedback, RPGs   *100042.400@compuserve.com*
Editor, rumors   *76276.2147@compuserve.com*
Frank Magazine, Ottawa, Ont.   *ag419@freenet.carleton.ca*
Focus, Munich, Germany   *100335.3131@compuserve.com*
Forbes   *5096930@mcimail.com*
Glamour   *glamourmag@aol.com*
Go World   *ishius@ishius.com*
GQ   *gqmag@aol.com*
Illinois Issues, Springfield, Ill.   *wojcicki@eagle.sangamon.edu.*
Inside Media   *mediaseven@aol.com*
InterFace Magazine, Victoria, BC   *jedi@dataflux.bc.ca*
Internal Medicine News, Rockville, Md.   *Cpierce@cpcug.org*
Journal of Irreproducible Results   *jir@mit.edu Cambridge, Mass.*
Kurier Chemiczny (Chemical Courier)   *kurier@chem.uw.edu.pl*

Medical Laboratory Observer
    Letters to the editor   *editor.mlo@medtechnet.com*
    Tips & Technlogy   *tips.mlo@medtechnet.com*
    Computer Dialog   *computer.mlo@medtechnet.com*
    Management   *management.mlo@medtechnet.com*
Midwifery Today & Childbirth Education   *midwifery@aol.com*
Mondo 2000   *mondo@well.com*
Mother Jones   *x@mojones.com*
Multichannel News   *higgins@dorsai.dorsai.org*
The Nation   *nation@igc.org*
The New Republic   *editors@tnr.com*
New Scientist, U.K. (U.S. Bureau)   *75310.1661@compuserve.com*
"The Last Word"   *newsc1@stirling.ac.uk*
Newsweek
    Letters to the editor   *letters@newsweek.com*
    Periscope   *71333.3401@compuserve.com*
NOW Magazine, Toronto   *news@now.com*
Oberlin Alumni Magazine   *alummag@ocvaxc.cc.oberlin.edu.*
Ob.Gyn. News, Rockville, Md.   *Cpierce@cpcug.org*
One Country, Baha'i International   *1country@bic.org*
Ottawa (Ont.) Magazine   *aq060@freenet.carleton.ca*
Ottawa (Ont.) Business Magazine   *aq060@freenet.carleton.ca*
OutNOW!, San Jose, Calif.   *Jct@netcom.com*
Pediatric News, Rockville, Md.   *Cpierce@cpcug.org*
Physicians's Office Laboratories (POL) Advisor
    Letters to the editor   *editor.pol.mlo@medtechnet.com*
    Problem Solver   *problem.pol.mlo@medtechnet.com*
Playboy   *edit@playboy.com*
    Playboy Forum   *forum@playboy.com*
    Dear Playboy   *dearpb@playboy.com*
Postepy Fizyki (Advances in Physics)   *postepy@fuw.edu.pl*
PolandThe Progressive, Madison, Wisc.   *Progmag@igc.apc.org*
Real Goods News   *realgood@well.sf.ca.us*
Reason   *70703.2152@compuserve.com*
Rolling Stone, New York   *rollingstone@echonyc.com*
Running Wild Magazine, Lincoln, Mass.   *Runwild@world.std.com*
St. Charles Countian, Missouri   *pacmosteve@aol.com*
S.F. Examiner Magazine   *sfxmag@mcimail.com*
Security Insider Report   *p00506@psilink.com*
Silueta, Santa Rosa, Calif.   *silueta@wave.sci.org*
Skin & Allergy News, Rockville, Md.   *Cpierce@cpcug.org*
Soundprint   *soundprt@jhuvms.hcf.jhu.edu*
Sky & Telescope, Cambridge, Mass.   *Skytel@cfa.harvard.edu*
Spectrum, New York, N.Y.   *n.hantman@ieee.org*
Der Spiegel, Germany   *100064.3164@compuserve.com*
Stern, Hamburg, Germany   *100125.1305@compuserve.com*
3D-Magazin, Germany   *3d-magazin@stereo.stgt.sub.org*
Time   *timeletter@aol.com*
Training Magazine, Minneapolis   *trainmag@aol.com*
Transitions, Univ. of Southern Indiana   *jwolf.ucs@smtp.usi.edu*

U. Magazine	*umag@well.sf.ca.us*
Ultramarathon Canada	*an346@freenet.carleton.ca*
Urb, Los Angeles	*urbmag@netcom.com*
USA Weekend	*usaweekend@aol.com*
U.S. News and World Report	*71154.1006@compuserve.com*
Utne Reader	*editor@utnereader.com*
Vogue	*vogue-mail@aol.com*
Washington Technology	*technews@access.digex.net*
West Countian, Missouri	*pacmosteve@aol.com*
Whole Earth Review	*wer@well.sf.ca.us*
Wired	*editor@wired.com*
Z, Sweden	*z.mag@zine.se*
Zielone Brygady (Green Brigades)	*zielbryg@gn.apc.org*

News/Media Services and Press Associations

Associated Press ("On the Net" Column)	*weisc@well.sf.ca.us*
TV Direct	*conus-dc@clark.net*
Cowles/SIMBA Media Daily	*simba02@aol.com*
Greenwire	*greenwre@apn.com*
Katolicka Agencja Informacyjna, Poland	*kai@ikp.atm.com.pl*
Media Page	*mpage@netcom.com*
M2 News Agency, U.K.	*satnews@cix.compulink.co.uk*
National Press Photographers Assn.	*Loundy@plink.geis.com*
Newsbytes	*newsbytes@genie.geis.com*
Telecomworldwire, U.K.	*satnews@cix.compulink.co.uk*

Radio and TV Networks

American Public Radio ("Marketplace")	*market@usc.edu*
BBC World Service	*iac@bbc-ibar.demon.co.uk*
CBC Radio, "Brand X"	*brandx@winnipeg.cbc.ca*
CBC Radio, "Brave New Waves"	*bnw@babylon.montreal.qc.ca*
CBS, "Late Show with David Letterman"	*lateshow@pipeline.com*
CNN Global News	*cnnglobal@aol.com*
C-SPAN (Requests for Coverage)	*cspanprogm@aol.com*
Questions during live call-ins	*cspanguest@aol.com*
Viewer services and questions	*cspanviewr@aol.com*
Channel 2, "Rapport," Sweden	*twonews@basys.svt.se*
Fox TV	*foxnet@delphi.com*
Maine Public TV, "Media Watch"	*greenman@maine.maine.edu*
Nebraska Educational TV, Lincoln, Neb.	*Etv@unlinfo.unl.edu*
NBC News, New York, N.Y.	*nightly@news.nbc.com*
"Dateline"	*dateline@news.nbc.com*
National Public Radio ("Talk of the Nation")	*totn@npr.org*
"Talk of the Nation/Sci.Friday"	*scifri@aol.com*
"Fresh Air"	*freshair@hslc.org*
"Weekend All Things Considered"	*watc@clark.net*
"Weekend Edition/Sunday"	*wesun@clark.net*
"West Coast Live"	*owner-west_coast_live@netcom.com*

Ohio University Public Radio	*radio@ohiou.edu*
Ohio University Public Television	*tv@ohiou.edu*
Polskie Radio Program I, Poland	*radio1@ikp.atm.com.pl*
Polska Telewizja Kablowa, Poland	*ptk@ikp.atm.com.pl*
PBS, "POV"	*povonline@aol.com*
"Radio Graffiti"	*alan@panix.com*
Rush Limbaugh Show	*70277.2502@compuserve.com*
TV Ontario, "The Future"	*the_future@tvo.org*
Voice of America/Worldnet Television	
From outside the U.S.	*letters@voa.gov*
From within the U.S.	*letters-usa@voa.gov*
QSL reports, outside U.S.	*qsl@voa.gov*
QSL reports, inside U.S.	*qsl-usa@voa.gov*
Agriculture Today	*agri@voa.gov*
VOA-Europe (English)	*voa-europe@voa.gov*
VOA-Morning Program	*voa-morning@voa.gov*

Radio and TV Stations

Radio Havana, Cuba ("DXers Unlimited")	*radiohc@tinored.cu*
KHOU-TV, Houston	*khou@neosoft.com*
KING-AM, Seattle	*king1090@aol.com*
KIRO-AM/FM, Seattle	*kiro@halcyon.com*
KKSF-FM and KDFC-AM/FM, San Francisco	
General comments	*comments@kksf.tbo.com*
News releases	*news@kksf.tbo.com*
KOMO-AM, Seattle	*normg@halcyon.com*
KOMU-TV, NBC, Columbia, Mo.	*swoelfel@bigcat.missouri.edu.*
KOIN, Portland, Ore.	*koin06A@prodigy.com*
KRON-TV, San Francisco	
Gardening segment	*garden4@aol.com*
KUAT-TV, PBS, Tucson, Ariz.	*comments@kuat.arizona.edu*
KUOW Radio, Seattle	*kuow@u.washington.edu*
KUSP-FM, Santa Cruz, Calif.	*Kusp@cruzio.com*
KWMU-FM, St. Louis, Mo.	*kwmu@umslva.bitnet*
KXTV-TV, Sacramento, Calif.	*Kxtv@netcom.com*
KZSU, Palo Alto, Calif.	*releases@kzsu.stanford.edu*
WBBM-TV, CBS, Chicago	*wbbmch2@aol.com*
WBFO-FM, NPR, Buffalo, N.Y.	*wbfo@ubvms.cc.buffalo.edu*
WBNQ-FM, Bloomington, Ill.	*radiobn@heartland.bradley.edu*
WCBS-AM, CBS, New York	*news88a@prodigy.com*
WCVB-TV, Boston, Mass.	*wcvb@aol.com*
WCCO-TV, Minneapolis, Minn.	*Wccotv@mr.net*
WDCB Radio, Glen Ellyn, Ill.	*scotwitt@interaccess.com*
WEOL-AM, Elyria, Ohio	*maweol@freenet.lorain.oberlin.edu.*
WEOS, Geneva, N.Y.	*weos@hws.bitnet*
WEEK-TV, Peoria, Ill.	*xxweek@heartland.bradley.edu*
WFAA-TV, ABC/CNN, Dallas/Ft. Worth, TX	
News department	*news8@onramp.net*
WFLA-AM, Tampa	*wfla97b@prodigy.com*

WFMJ-TV, Youngstown, Ohio	*news21a@yfn.ysu.edu*
WGN-TV, Chicago	*wgntv@aol.com*
WHDH-TV, CBS, Boston	*74201.2255@compuserve.com*
WHO-AM, Des Moines, Iowa	*news@who-radio.com*
WICB, Ithaca, N.Y.	*wicb@aol.com*
WISH-TV, CBS, Indianapolis, Ind.	*Wish08b@prodigy.com*
WJBC-AM, Bloomington, Ill.	*radiobn@heartland.bradley.edu*
WMBR-FM, Cambridge, Mass.	
Listener mail	*wmbr@athena.mit.edu*
News/Political Releases	*wmbr-press@media.mit.edu*
WNWV-FM, Elyria, Ohio	*maweol@freenet.lorain.oberlin.edu.*
WNYC, "On the Line," New York	*76020.560@compuserve.com*
WRCT-FM, Pittsburgh, Pa.	*wrct@andrew.cmu.edu*
WRVU-FM, Oswego, N.Y.	*wrvu@oswego.edu*
WSRN-AM, Cedarville, Ohio	*wsrn@cedarnet.cedarville.edu*
WTVF-TV, Nashville, Tenn.	*sysop@newschannel5.com*
WVIT-TV, New Britain, Conn	*wvit30a@prodigy.com*
WWWE-AM Cleveland, Ohio	*talk11a@prodigy.com*
WXYZ-TV, ABC, Detroit	*wxyztv@aol.com*
WYDE-AM, "Tony Giles," Birmingham	*tony.giles@the-matrix.com*

Computer Publications

Best of Mac News, Belgium	*best.of@applelink.apple.com*
Boardwatch, Colorado Springs, Colo.	*Letters@boardwatch.com*
CD-ROM World	*meckler@jvnc.net*
Communications News	*489–8359@mcimail.com*
Corporate Computing	*439–3854@mcimail.com*
Communications Networks, U.K.	*75300.243@compuserve.com*
Communications Week	*440–7485@mcimail.com*
Computer Shopper, U.K. only	*100034.1056@compuserve.com*
Computer Weekly, U.K.	*Comp_weekly@cix.compulink.co.uk*
ComputerWorld	*letters@cw.com*
Computing, U.K.	*computed@cix.compulink.co.uk*
Data Communications	*416–2157@mcimail.com*
Datateknik, Sweden	*datateknik@dt.etforlag.se*
DBMS	*73647.2767@compuserve.com*
EE Times	*70212.14@compuserve.com*
Enterprise Systems Journal	*543–3256@mcimail.com*
Home Office Computing	*hoc@aol.com*
IBM Internet Journal, Dallas, Tex.	*76130.221@compuserve.com*
InfoLinja, Finland	*jlahti@infocrea.fi*
Information Week	*informationweek@mcimail.com*
Infoworld	*letters@infoworld.com*
The Internet Business Journal	*mstrange@fonorola.net*
The Internet Letter	*netweek@access.digex.net*
Internet World	*meckler@jvnc.neti*
X, Germany	*post@ix.de*
Journal of C Language Translation	*ljclt@iecc.com*
LAN Times	*538–6488@mcimail.com*

MACLine, Philadelphia   *macline1@aol.com*
Macworld   *macworld@aol.com*
MacTech Magazine (formerly MacTutor)
  Press releases   *pressreleases@xplain.com*
  Orders, Circ., Customer Service   *custservice@xplain.com*
  Editorial   *editorial@xplain.com*
  Publisher   *publisher@xplain.com*
  Ad sales   *adsales@xplain.com*
  Programmers Challenge   *progchallenge@xplain.com*
  Accounting   *accounting@xplain.com*
  Marketing   *marketing@xplain.com*
  General   *info@xplain.com*
MicroTimes   *microx@well.sf.ca.us*
Network Computing   *editor@nwc.com*
Network World   *network@world.std.com*
Reader Advocacy Force   *nwraf@world.std.com*
Online Access   *oamag@aol.com*
OS/2 Developer, Delray Beach, Fla.   *Os2mag@vnet.ibm.com*
PC Magazine   *157–9301@mcimail.com*
PC Plus, U.K.   *pcplus@cix.compulink.co.uk*
PC Week   *557–0379@mcimail.com*
Personal Computer World, U.K.   *editorial@pcw.ccmail.compuserve.com*
Telecommunications   *311–1693@mcimail.com*
UniForum Monthly   *pubs@uniforum.org*
UniNews   *pubs@uniforum.org*
UnixWorld
  News releases/breaking news   *news@uworld.com*
  European news (European)   *euro@uworld.com*
  Product info   *products@uworld.com*
  To get a product reviewed   *reviews@uworld.com*
  Calendar listings (4 months lead)   *cal@uworld.com*
  Letters to the editor   *letters@uworld.com*
  Writer information   *write@uworld.com*
  Tutorial information   *rik@uworld.com*
  Wiz Grabbag   *grabbag@uworld.com*
  Answers to Unix submissions   *ans2unix@uworld.com*
  Subscription info   *circ@uworld.com*
Xephon, U.K.   *100325.3711@compuserve.com*

Newsletters

Accountants on Line   *ayfdave@aol.com*
Africalink, Philadelphia   *sern@aol.com*
Aviation Daily, Washington, D.C.   *grahamg@mgh.com*
Card Systems   *satnews@cix.compulink.co.uk*
China Business and Economic Update   *chinahand@aol.com*
Data Broadcasting News, U.K.   *satnews@cix.compulink.co.uk*
Dealmakers   *Ted.Kraus@property.com*
Ecologia, Lithuania   *root@jt.aiva.lt*
Electronic Marketplace Report   *simba02@aol.com*

Information Law Alert	*markvoor@phantom.com*
Infosecurity News	*2439796@mcimail.com*
Multimedia Business Report	*simba02@aol.com*
NewsInc	*simba02@aol.com*
New Business Watch, Sebastopol, Calf.	*70307.454@Compuserve.com*
Satnews	*satnews@cix.compulink.co.uk*
Security Insider Report	*p00506@psilink.com*
The Small Business Gazette, New York	*jimd34@aol.com*
Smart's California Insurance Bulletin	*0005068090@mcimail.com*
Smart's Calif. Workers' Comp Bulletin	*0005068090@mcimail.com*
Smart's National Comp & Health Bull.	*0005068090@Mcimail.com*
Smart's Excess & Surplus Bulletin	*0005068090@mcimail.com*
Society of Newspaper Design	*fairbairn@plink.geis.com*
Spec-Com Journal	*spec-com@genie.geic.com*

Common Emoticons

In general, I would recommend that you not use these "smileys" in your online communications. Although they are fairly common, not enough people know what they mean. They can confuse many of your readers. But because people are including emoticons like these in *their* messages *to* you, you'll want to know what some of the more popular ones signify (tilt your head to the left to see most of these symbols):

:)	happy face
: -)	smiling or laughing
: (	unhappy
: - o	shocked
: -	undecided or uncommitted

You may also run into acronyms online. Here are some popular ones:

BTW	"By the way"
IMHO	"In my humble opinion"
<g>	"grin"
IRL	"In real life"
ROFL	"Rolling on floor laughing"

Finally, there are new online words being coined every day. I would not suggest using these in your writing, either. They are very obscure. For example:

cyberlinguidiot: A marketing executive who adds techie
                   prefixes (like "cyber") to words to
                   make them sound hi-tech
dirt road: An unusually slow link
JPIG: Site or page containing a large number
                   of images that drastically increase load-
                   ing time

Suggested Readings

Although there are hundreds of books about writing, marketing, and cyberspace, and hundreds more to come, these are the best of the crop, IMHO. For current reviews of other relevant books, see **http://arganet.tenagra.com/books.html.**

Angell, David, and Brent Heslop. *The Elements of E-mail Style.* Reading, Mass.: Addison-Wesley, 1994.

Blake, Gary, and Robert W. Bly. *The Elements of Business Writing.* New York: Macmillan, 1991.

Caples, John. *Tested Advertising Methods.* Englewood Cliffs, N.J.: Prentice-Hall, 1996.

Emery, Vince. *How to Grow Your Business on the Internet.* Scottsdale, Ariz.: Coriolis Group, 1995.

Gelormine, Vince. *The Internet Marketing Black Book.* Fort Lauderdale, Fla.: Legion Publishing, 1995.

Hogan, Kevin. *The Psychology of Persuasion.* New Orleans: Pelican, 1996.

Hopkins, Claude C. *My Life in Advertising* and *Scientific Advertising* (combined in one volume). Chicago: NTC Business Books, 1990.

Horrigan, Alice. *Your Guide to Effective Internet Ad and Brochure Writing.* GEC Publishers, 1994. (Available from P.O. Box 1948, Brookline, Mass. 02146.)

Keeler, Len. CyberMarketing. New York: AMACOM, 1995.

Levinson, Jay Conrad, and Charles Rubin. *Guerilla Marketing Online.* Boston: Houghton Mifflin, 1995.

Mulkern, Thomas. *Online Marketing Action Plan.* Pathfinder Publishing, 1994. (Available only from 17 Pleasant St., Andover, Mass. 01810.)

Ogilvy, David. *Confessions of an Advertising Man.* New York: Ballantine, 1963.

Resnick, Rosalind, and Dave Taylor. *The Internet Business Guide: Riding the Information Superhighway to Profit.* Indianapolis: Sams Publishing, 1994.

Schwab, Victor O. *How to Write a Good Advertisement: A Short Course in Copywriting.* North Hollywood, Cal.: Wilshire Book Co., 1962.

Shea, Virginia. *Netiquette.* San Francisco: Albion Books, 1994.

Vitale, Joe. *The AMA Complete Guide to Small Business Advertising.* Chicago: NTC, 1995.

————. *The Seven Lost Secrets of Success.* Ashland, Ohio: VistaTron, 1992.

————. *Turbocharge Your Writing!* Houston: Awareness Publications, 1988.

Yudkin, Marcia. *Marketing Online.* New York: Plume, 1995. *The Internet Resource Quick Reference. Indianapolis: Que Corporation, 1994.*

Index

About the Author

Joe "Mister Fire!" Vitale may be the world's first "CyberCopy-writer."

He runs an advertising, marketing and promotion agency in Houston, Texas. He is the author of seven books, including *Turbocharge Your Writing!* (Awareness Publications, 1988), *The Seven Lost Secrets of Success* (VistaTron, 1992), *Hypnotic Writing* (Awareness Publications, 1993), and *The AMA Complete Guide to Small Business Advertising* (NTC Business Books, 1995). He is a highly sought-after copywriter, speaker, and marketing specialist. To receive his free newsletter, e-mail him at:

mrfire@blkbox.com

or

jgvitale@ix.netcom.com.

Or visit his Copywriting Profit Center at **http://www.bookfair.com/welcome/cyberwriter/new.**